RENEWING HARVEST:
CELEBRATING GOD'S CREATION

Renewing Harvest:
Celebrating God's Creation

Craig Millward

The Pentland Press Limited
Edinburgh · Cambridge · Durham · USA

© Craig Millward 2001

First published in 2001 by
The Pentland Press Ltd.
1 Hutton Close
South Church
Bishop Auckland
Durham

British Library Cataloguing in Publication Data.
A catalogue record for this book is available
from the British Library.

ISBN 1 85821 925 6

Typeset by George Wishart & Associates, Whitley Bay.
Printed and bound by Antony Rowe Ltd., Chippenham.

Acknowledgements

This book began life in the classroom, and as an MA thesis. I am therefore grateful to Tim Marks for his enthralling Doctrine of Creation lectures, and to my various MA tutors for the ideas that were originally theirs.

I also thank Graham Dale for suggesting that renewing the Harvest Festival was an ideal way of giving practical expression to my earlier thoughts. My friend Bob Carling has also been a constant source of advice and encouragement.

Contents

Chapter Four: The Promise of Redemption

Chapter 5: Harvest – The Festival of Creation

Dedication

I dedicate this book to my wife Andrea, and to our two children Shaun and Bethany. As we discover more of God's grace together it gives me hope that the whole earth will one day discover the liberation that we are struggling to live out in our lives together.

I also write in memory of our Old English Sheepdog, Muttley who died in October 1997 and in appreciation of Rusty who has more than replaced him! Animal companions can teach us so much about the value of life and how to enjoy it.

Finally, I am thankful to the many people who have provoked me to think and inspired me to write those thoughts down on paper. I also thank the supervisors who helped with this material when it began life as an MA thesis, and the members of Shirley Baptist Church and Ormesby Baptist Church who I have served as Pastor and have supported me in my desire to see the 'sons of God' take their rightful place as faithful stewards of all God has entrusted to us.

Foreword

Week by week, Christians profess faith in the God who is Creator and Redeemer of the world. We pray to the God who made all things; we affirm a creed that declares God as the maker of heaven and earth.

However, the world we live in is not only the product of God's good creation. It is the result of humankind's failure to care for creation responsibly. We face an ecological crisis.

Craig's book is written with this crisis in mind. He is concerned for a proper Christian approach to the environment within which we find life and upon which we depend. He explores the major biblical themes of creation, the fall, covenant, and redemption, and examines each one with this concern in mind. So he seeks to help us towards greater ecological wisdom, rooted in scripture and in our theological tradition.

Craig finishes by rooting this theology in action, calling us to rediscover the power and meaning of Harvest Festival and to act as churches for the renewal of the earth.

No one should need reminding about the contemporary importance of this issue as we enter a new millennium. Too often theology has been used to justify the abuse and misuse of creation. We need to hear and receive a theology, grounded in scripture, that challenges us to work for the renewal of creation in the name of the God who made all things good.

David Coffey
General Secretary of the Baptist Union of Great Britain

Introduction

Since 1873, when the concept of ecology[1] first appeared in the English language, an active interest in the environment began to establish itself in Western thought. The arrival of the 'science' of ecology made it possible to begin quantifying the effects that past and present human activities were having on other species and upon the health of the planet as a whole; and this new understanding provided humankind with the tools and the impetus with which to evaluate the often radical and permanent ways in which the environment had been adapted and changed.

In 1967, an article was written which explored the relationship between this concern for the environment and Judeo-Christian theology. The article in question was written by the American historian Lynn White Jr., and was to become one of the standard works of reference for environmentalists in general, and for Christians with an interest in the environment in particular.[2] In it, White made the simple observation that human beings are, by virtue of their superior power and intelligence, the greatest living modifiers of the environment. In assuming this role, human beings have been able to initiate radical ecological changes, which they have only recently been able (and even more recently willing) to quantify and evaluate. In the meantime, delicate natural balances are being altered, and each choice that is made in setting the course of human destiny on this planet has a resultant impact upon the living environment that future generations will inherit.

The article identified two major forces within Western

society: science and technology. White then observed that both of these, in their modern form, are distinctly Western, and the values that underlie them were shaped long before the Scientific and Industrial Revolutions. These are the twin beliefs that progress is inevitable, and that humans are the natural exploiters of nature. What makes these views distinctly Western, according to White, is that they both have their roots in a Judeo-Christian world view. The Bible has a linear view of history as opposed to the Eastern cyclical view, and teaches an anthropocentric creation history in which humans are the God-ordained masters of creation. White believed this implies that nature exists for no reason other than to serve humanity.

Furthermore, not only did these values make the rise of science and technology possible in the West, but they also played their part in determining the direction these advances were to take. White believes that it was the mixture of such a strong doctrine of progress with these exploitative and anthropocentric ideas that led to an oppressive Western ethos which submerged other cultures and destroyed gentler world views in its path of progress.

White therefore laid a heavy burden of responsibility at the feet of Christian theology, both citing it as being the major reason behind the history of ecological crisis, and also looking to its reformation for any real hope of progress. It might seem strange to turn for help to the very 'beast' that makes reformation necessary, but White does so because he believed that Western culture has imbibed Christian values so deeply that any hope of its adopting a completely different culture is impossible. He is by no means alone in this belief: John Passmore, who does not attribute as much blame to Christian theology as White does, writes:

> Important changes in moral outlook can occur, have occurred; in producing . . . changes, individual reformers, whether statesmen or prophets, have played an important part. But the degree to

which their reforms have in the long run been successful depends upon the degree to which they have been able to appeal to and further develop already existing traditions.[3]

White therefore looks to the Christian Church to provide a lead in re-thinking the foundational principles upon which Western society views the environment. Although he sees the need more in terms of a *re-invention* of ideas based upon the same foundation, I will argue that a *rediscovery* is more in order. I hope the reasons for this will become clear as the book progresses, and as I follow many others in taking up the gauntlet White threw down to Christian theology more than a quarter of a century ago. Unfortunately Christians have rarely been at the forefront of the creation care lobby – perhaps because since our task is essentially 'spiritual', and about the redemption of fallen humans, we have therefore seen God's creation as less important, or the kind of thing pagans or 'New Agers' get interested in. More commonly we have become too caught up in other things to spare the time.

The bible's message has remained unchanged for countless generations. This book highlights the fact that the earth in which we live was deliberately created by God to be good, and was intended to remain a fruitful blessing to be farmed and developed by man for the good of the whole creation. The state of this earth has therefore never been an afterthought to our creator. It is humanity's failure to recognize that the world around us is precious to God, and is to be cared for and conserved for its own sake as well as ours, that has reflected both our self-preoccupation and our tendency only to follow those maker's instructions which we judge fit to obey.

I have chosen to tackle this subject in a unique way. It seems that, up until now, most Christian writers have either explored and evaluated the contribution of a single theological tradition to a theology of the environment; or they have taken a collection of environmental issues and applied biblical injunctions to them in an attempt to elicit a biblical response. This has been, largely, very helpful. However, I have preferred to begin with the biblical text and consider what it has to say about God's creation and human responsibility under four major headings – The Story of Creation, The Meaning of the Fall, God's Covenant with Creation and The Hope of Redemption.

The Story of Creation is primarily about God as creator. It demonstrates both God's rule over all things and his concern to sustain all that he has made. Christian Theology is too often influenced either by Platonic thought which splits everything up into an ordered hierarchical structure in which the divine or 'spiritual' is valued and aspired to and the material is spurned; or by pantheistic theories which subsume God within creation – often to the extent that he is not allowed to be transcendent at all. In my examination of the biblical texts I examine the relationship between God and creation, and show that creation is the result of a unique creative act by a God who is distinct from all he has made – but at the same time is involved with it and cares for it. So God's affirmation that all he has made is good is important, as is his pledge to continue to sustain his creation.

I then move on to consider the creation of mankind, and find that by far the most dominant theme is the fact that together we have been created in the image of God. Through-out the ages we have applied this metaphor to ourselves as a badge of god-likeness and have assumed an air of superiority and the role of ruler over creation. But this image, given by God and part of what makes us human, in fact focuses more upon God than upon itself or its bearer. So it is impossible to understand its meaning correctly without first appreciating the purpose for which it was given.

The bible tells us that the primary reasons we were created in God's image were so that we could enjoy a relationship with our creator, and so that we should fulfil our God-given mandate to rule the earth as God's priests – standing between God and creation and representing one to the other in the manner of a shepherd who is concerned to ensure that his flock find safe pasture. Over all this, God reveals himself not as an absentee landlord who is unconcerned as to the fate that befalls his property, but as a loving creator whose beloved creation has estranged itself from his tender care.

The story of the Fall indicates that when Adam and Eve lost their relationship with God and were cast out of paradise this had a variety of long term effects. The loss of fellowship with God has affected the way we view ourselves, and also affects our relationships with our fellow man and with creation. Furthermore, our understanding of our potentiality and our destiny was also marred; as is the creation itself which, in its groaning state, no longer knows the care of its creator as it once did. The earth thus became man's enemy, and the animals cowered in fear of this new and powerful beast amongst them. Adam and his descendants then began to seek to overpower their environment – showing that although our calling to care for the earth remained intact; this was now going to be an impossibility as long as man remained his own master. This is where we now find ourselves – for although we are aware of a multitude of needs – many of which threaten our own survival, our continued shortsightedness and greed seem to render us powerless to do anything to save ourselves.

But God does not give up on his fallen world. In his consistent and persistent love God reinitiates the covenant he made with the earth at creation, and sets out a list of wise rules in order to provide for ordered and secure relationships within fallen creation. And within both the covenant and the law God includes rights for land and animals as well as humans. The unmistakeable message of the Covenant is that God still intends mankind to fulfil the functions we were given at creation, and to that extent we remain entrusted with dominion over our world. But, as fallen beings, we too often misunderstand or neglect our calling. I spend time exploring what the themes of dominion and rule mean and discover that no matter which angle we view the command from, the way we treat the earth today is neither just nor right. Thus the suggestion that God's ordering of creation is a license to exploit or dominate it shows that we have completely misunderstood the creator's instructions and intentions.

But the doctrine of redemption shines as a beacon of hope. God has not given up on us or his creation, and his promise to redeem all things provides us with the basis of real hope for the future. But just as it is a mistake to focus wholly on the human dimension of redemption, it is also an incomplete response to suggest that it is possible to save the earth without addressing man's responsibility for its current state. Redemption begins with man, because sin began with man. So it is only as a right view of ourselves and our place within the universe is restored to us that we can be set free to act rightly towards creation. This redemption is both personal, in that it calls for each individual to make a repentant response; and cosmic – brought only by the risen and returning Christ – because however hard we try we will never be able to restore the peace we stole from our fellow created beings. That is still to be awaited, and will be brought about when the saviour of the earth makes all things new.

It is the final chapter on Harvest that is probably the most important of all, since as God's stewards, Christians are the 'sons of God' upon whom creation is waiting to teach the ungodly how to live (Rom. 8). But we desperately need to find some way of re-focusing our attention on issues of Creation Care in the way that the Old Testament festivals did. I suggest that the best way to do this would be to rejuvenate our Harvest Festival and enable it to become the primary means by which we get back in touch with our call to be wise stewards of creation. I provide many practical examples of ways in which this might be done and also provide information as to where further resources can be found.

Notes

1. Defined as: 'The study of the relationships between living organisms and their environment' – *The Collins English Dictionary*.

2. Lynn White Jr. – 'The Historical Roots of our Ecologic Crisis.' Published in *Science*. Vol. 155 No 3767. 10th March 1967.

3. John Passmore – *Man's Responsibility for Nature: Ecological problems and Western Traditions*. (Scribner. New York. 1974) p 40.

CHAPTER ONE

~

The Story of Creation

The Creation of the World

The story of creation is central to the Christian faith. Its important place in Christian theology is reflected in its pride of place at the beginning of both the Apostles' creed (AD 390) and the Nicene Creed (AD 381), both of which are early examples of Christian orthodoxy. Its place in these creeds reflects the fact that:

> the Hebrew people came to a faith in creation neither through a philosophical analysis of the origin of things nor through a search for a First Cause. On the contrary, they found God as he acted in history and it was because they were convinced that God is the Lord of all nations that they were led to see that he is the creator.[1]

Throughout the early centuries of the Christian era, the story of creation was implicitly believed by Christians and rarely questioned. Perhaps this is because in a climate where knowledge about the world was relatively limited, believers found it natural to see God as the explanation of those areas of the world that were outside of human understanding and thus to equate God with the sum total of human ignorance.[2] As long as the gaps in human knowledge remained vast it was perhaps natural to interpret the biblical accounts as accurate records of creation history without possibility of contradiction. But the passage of the centuries and the resulting increase in human knowledge demanded that this central belief in God as creator be subjected to philosophical analysis. This gave rise to questions regarding the extent to which God is still involved in his creation, and debates about God as First Cause, *Creatio ex*

Nihilo (Creation out of nothing)[3] etc., all of which we will consider in due course.

Although each age produced its critics who challenged dogma based on literalist interpretations of the bible, it was the 1500s that brought the 'Copernican Watershed' when Copernicus and Galileo were challenged by a church which believed that scripture could be relied upon to settle questions of scientific belief. Both Copernicus and Galileo were Roman Catholics, and neither denied that the bible contained physical truths. But their work had led them to discover that, in the words of Galileo, 'the intention of the Holy Ghost is to teach us how one goes to heaven, not how heaven goes'[4] The church was not to heed this advice and from this time observation and experiment began to replace uncritical acceptance of tradition. The slow squeeze continued until, several centuries later, the most sustained attack on the literal reading of the creation narratives began with the publication of Sir Charles Lyell's book *Principles of Geology* (1830-33). Lyell believed that his study of rocks and fossils revealed that the Earth's crust was not brought to its present state through one 'creation moment', but through millennia of gradual change. This implied that the world had to be much older than many theologians had previously thought. Up until this time, the common view was that the bible described a world that was created just 6,000 years previously; whereas Lyell's discoveries suggested that it was anything up to 200 million years old. Although a number of clever theories arose to square Lyell's work with this traditional understanding of Genesis, the tide was only held back for 30 years until Charles Darwin published his book *On the Origin of Species by Natural Selection* in 1859.

In it, Darwin revised and expanded the theory that individuals within a species might slowly change, eventually becoming a new species. But Darwin, unlike Robert Chambers before him, seemed to array such a mass of evidence to support his theory, that it was impossible for the world to ignore his findings. If Lyell had challenged assumptions about the age of the earth, Darwin's theories seemed to subvert the idea of design – thus weakening Paley's case for a 'Natural Theology'.[5] So when taken together, these two theories suggested to many that life might not have appeared on earth in the way a literal reading of Genesis indicated – raising questions about whether the widely trusted literal interpretation of Genesis was sustainable; and even whether Lyell and Darwin had eliminated the need for God within the creation equation. Darwin, perhaps unwittingly, added to this feeling when, as his theory developed, he gradually allowed his use of metaphors such as 'Nature' to become absolutized – eventually taking the same roles as Paley's concept of God.[6] It is interesting to note at this point that it was those who possessed the 'strongest *a priori* commitment to the authority of the bible . . . who offered the *least* opposition to Darwin'.[7] Indeed James Moore concludes 'it was only those who maintained a distinctly orthodox theology who could embrace Darwinism'[8] since the debate involved no new issues of principle, and they had learned from Galileo that scripture was not intended to be a scientific textbook.[9] Russell concludes that:

> it was not that they failed to take Scripture properly into account. Because they took it so seriously they declined to saddle it with arbitrary interpretations that flew in the face of empirical evidence.[10]

The fact is that, in time, theologians such as Aubrey Moore found it possible to welcome these theories as 'fresh matter for adoring the power and wisdom of God,'[11] but this appropriation took a great deal of time and left many behind.[12]

During this time theologians set about the task of redefining traditional theological understanding. The beginnings of this reappraisal came when Friedrich Schleiermacher provided the foundations for a Christianity that was founded on 'natural theology'.[13] Schleiermacher came to agree with those in the romantic movement who saw religious 'experience' as being the most direct way of knowing God. So for him, any faith that was centred in a series of morals or laws was partial and necessarily limited because knowledge of God could only come through reason and experience.

This led the way for the 'liberals', who in their attempt to adapt Christian theology to make it acceptable to the Western scientific mind built on the work of proponents of natural religion like Friedrich Schleiermacher and existentialists such as Søren Kierkegaard. They too insisted that experience, and not evidence, should be the primary means of evaluating Christian doctrine. So, Albrecht Ritschl wrote about a Jesus who was simply the 'perfect man' who succeeded in changing humanity's attitude to God; thus making it possible for the human race to evolve steadily towards perfection,[14] and C.W. Goodwin said that 'the story of creation should be regarded as a simple Hebrew myth adapted to the needs of those to whom it was written.'[15] Rudolf Bultmann was later to build on these foundations with his quest to demythologize traditional Christian theology.

The result of this onslaught was that the church, which had never had to defend itself on these fronts before, was unsure about whether to allow these new ideas space to develop alongside its more traditional theology. Claus Westermann believes that during this period the church abandoned the doctrine of creation to the scientists. Up until this time of rapidly expanding understanding about the world in which we lived, a God who was the sum of the gaps in our understanding had been immense and awesome. As human knowledge grew, and the gaps shrunk, the implication seemed to be that God was becoming smaller. Then as scientists pointed to the possibility of greater and greater control over the human environment the role of any concept of God also became peripheral and, for many, unnecessary. The realization that it was too simplistic to make God equal to the sum total of human ignorance came too late to offer any meaningful apologetic; and for those who felt it necessary to defend the faith in order to retain its orthodoxy the only option was a retreat into fundamentalist literalism.[16]

Thus it was insisted by the literalists that Genesis chapters 1 and 2 contained a textbook-like account of *how* the world was created, and various theories grew up to help this stand appeal to the rational mind.[17] The problem was that in a world which was now offered a choice between the findings of science that could be tested and observed, and the teachings of a church which seemed determined to cling to some unnecessary interpretations of scripture in order to defend itself against internal strife, Christian theology became less relevant and credible. So in an age in which it was taught that the findings of science contradicted the biblical account of creation; it became impossible to build a bridge between science and faith. The result was that these essential chapters of Genesis were associated most commonly with those fundamentalists who, convinced that God had left us with a literal blow by blow account of *how* he brought the world into being, put up the shutters and were not prepared either to consider other ideas which contradicted their world view, or to engage in the kind of critical debate which might have exposed some of the weaknesses of Darwin's theories.

The result of all this was that the story of Creation became marginalized and discredited. It was used as a shield by Christians who felt under attack, and was ridiculed by others who were convinced that it lacked any value. The result of this battle was that we lost the emphasis the creation story places upon a relationship between an omnipotent creator-God and his creation, and the void was filled by an increased sense of human self-consciousness and self-importance.

Even before this marginalizing of the creation story, the preferred understanding of the relationship between human and non-human creation came from neo-Platonist theologians like Augustine and Aquinas who insisted that the human and rational took precedence over the 'merely' material. Now, with the creation story misunderstood and misrepresented, this low view of nature became accepted as the biblical view.

Without doubt, the most important foundation stone of Western theology was laid at the time of the Reformation. But with Martin Luther's important rediscovery of the doctrine of Justification by Faith also came a further, unintended, shift towards individualism and human centredness. Allied with this rediscovery of human freedom to relate to God on an individual basis were the teachings of Jean Calvin. Having swept into Geneva in 1541 on a tide of popular acclaim he began to elucidate his doctrine of predestination. In it he insisted that God had chosen who would be saved. This exercising of divine choice implied that those chosen were especially favoured by God and that the remainder had been 'chosen' for punishment. There was no place for the non-human creation within this system. Calvinists were later to insist that since God had made his choice, human endeavour on behalf of the 'lost' was pointless too. Later adherents also taught that since salvation was secure, and therefore not dependent upon right behaviour, humanity could act with impunity towards nature which was not the subject of God's promise and therefore thought to have little value.

These ideas are continued in many Puritan works which indicate that, having lost the ability to view the doctrine of salvation holistically, they became so preoccupied with individual human salvation that their doctrine of the Fall was almost wholly centred around the sin of the individual against God.[18] In a climate in which Sir Isaac Newton was propounding the theory that the earth was a vast clockwork mechanism with no value other than to serve humanity, and Christian theologians found it hard to see the creation narratives as any more than a factual account of how the world came about; God became relegated to merely 'first cause',[19] and any understanding of what God as the creator and sustainer of all that he had made might mean was quickly lost.

We will now revisit the creation story in the confidence that it forms part of God's revelation to mankind, and with the aim of discovering whether there is such thing as an ecological doctrine of creation which might now help us so many years after the creation story was written as we are faced with the task of looking after a world that seems to be falling apart around our ears. As we do so we will explore the important phrases in the Creation story, bearing in mind the following conclusions of Gerhard von Rad in his commentary on Genesis:

> Anyone who expounds Genesis ch. 1, must understand one thing: this chapter is priestly doctrine – indeed, it contains the essence of priestly knowledge in a most concentrated form. It was not 'written' once upon a time; but, rather, it is doctrine that has been carefully enriched over centuries by very slow growth. Nothing is here by chance; everything must be considered carefully, deliberately, and precisely. It is false, therefore, to reckon here even occasionally with archaic and half-mythological rudiments, which one considers venerable, to be sure, but theologically and conceptually less binding. What is said here is intended to hold true entirely and exactly as it stands. There is no trace of the hymnic element in the language, nor is anything said ... whose deeper meaning has to be deciphered. The exposition must painstakingly free this compact and rather esoteric doctrine sentence by sentence, indeed, word by word. These sentences cannot be easily over-interpreted theologically! Indeed, to us the danger appears greater that the expositor will fall short of discovering the concentrated doctrinal content.[20]

9

The Meaning of Creation

'In the beginning,' according to the first verse of the Genesis account, 'God created the heavens and the earth.'[21] This first sentence of the bible is dominated by two nouns. God (as subject) and the creation as the object of his creative attention and genius. What is most immediately striking here is that in the very beginning, the God who has no beginning and no end and is outside time, set history in motion by bringing the earth into being. The implication of this is that the omniscient creator of the universe knew from that first creative act what the finished product was to become and that although the cosmos was clearly distinct from its creator, it was fashioned in such a way as to remain both related to him and representative of him.[22]

The subject of the first sentence is God. This serves notice that the writers' intention is to reveal more about *who* created than what his command brought forth, and that this creator was also the owner and ruler of his creation. The concept of ruler is especially important in this study because it necessarily supposes an on-going relationship between creator and created; and powerfully refutes the teachings of the deist philosophers of the eighteenth century who taught that God was the watchmaker who had wound up his creation and then abandoned it whilst he presumably left his cosmic experiment and went on to other things. Here we have the beginnings of a true 'creator God' who is responsible for, and ruler over, the whole created order.

The involvement of God as central character in creation also has the effect of assuring the reader of his on-going involvement with all he has made. Millard Erickson shows how the writers of the Old Testament found it inconceivable that their understanding of a creator-God allowed room for any chance happenings. Even a phrase such as 'It rained' was impossible to interpret as meaning that the rain simply happened. To them, every event was a result of the providence of God.[23] This provides the foundation for the belief that *every* event that happens within creation is known to God because it is still dependent upon him for its very happening.[24] This God, the 'unargued cause' who cannot be proved and 'lies outside the realm of possible investigation,'[25] has, nevertheless, given rise to a great deal of philosophical and theological debate. This has produced two major questions, both of which are relevant to us here. The first asks why God created the heavens and the earth, and the second concerns the present relationship of the creator with his creation.

Why Did God Create the Heavens and the Earth?

Although the question might seem irrelevant, it is of extreme importance as we consider the impact of the creation story on environmental theology. Unless we have even the bones of an answer it will be difficult to proceed to suggest what the purpose and future of creation might be; assuming of course that what I have just suggested is true, and that the creator is still involved with it. If there is no reason behind creation it is logical to suppose that there is no secure future either – indeed we have no place referring to 'creation' at all. In that case we are cast adrift in a sea of nihilism. The question is also important for another reason, for, as George Hendry observes,

> If the mystery of creation is intensified to total ignorance, the profession of faith is reduced to a profession of agnosticism. – as when the expression 'God knows' is used in vulgar speech as a substitute for 'No one knows.' If faith in God as the creator of the world does not carry with it some understanding of creation that contains at least the possibility of an answer to the question Why? the confession is vacuous.[26]

The question 'Why did God create?' can be approached from one of two angles. The first follows the writings of Plato, who believed that at the heart of the answer lies the essential goodness of God. If God is good, he surmised, and in keeping with his goodness wishes to share himself with others, it is obvious that the act most in keeping with his nature would be to create an entity distinct from himself in order that he might communicate his goodness to it.[27]

The second approach begins with the supposition that there is an essential incompleteness within God's nature that *needed* to create the world in order to be filled. This view is most popularly found within the Process Theology of Alfred North Whitehead, which holds that 'God is not sufficient to himself without the world.'[28] Some might find it difficult to incorporate this into Christian theology if they feel uneasy about departing from the traditional view that since God is self-sufficient, it is therefore impossible for God to become *more* complete.

Although I have presented these two views as opposites, the two theories actually have a similar root, since as George Hendry comments, 'If God created the world in order to relieve a superfluity in his being, this would seem to mean that he acted under necessity, just as much as if he created the world in order to repair a deficiency in his being.'[29] However, elsewhere in the bible we note an understanding that God is the Lord and ruler of creation whose choice to create contained no element of compulsion.[30] This suggests that a new answer is needed. Francis Schaeffer's contribution to the debate is to assert that the solution begins with the doctrine of the Trinity which, since it ensures that completeness already existed within the Godhead, allows God to create from a position of strength rather than weakness.[31] Gerhard von Rad explains how the creative Word of God is sufficiently different to the human word, which would enable God to create in a completely free manner. It seems then that God's choice to create came out of an overflow of trinitarian love and, in the words of St Maximus the Confessor, a *'manicos eros'* – an unrequited, and even ecstatic love in which God creates the universe outside of himself. For it to have been any other way would, as von Rad insists, be contrary to divine freedom.[32]

The reason we have difficulty comprehending why God created all things, according to these commentators, is that the complete answer to the question 'Why did God create?' lies outside the realm of human understanding. Perhaps the human mind finds it impossible to imagine how an activity as important as creation can have entirely selfless beginnings, because such a fallen mind is unable to understand the nature of perfect love. Maybe we also need to recognize that whenever we are describing God our human vocabulary will always be of limited value. In order to begin from the Platonic angle then, it is essential that we first accept that the ways of God cannot always be explained by human reason. Indeed it may be further argued that it is only when we appreciate that God is able to act in a perfectly loving way which is outside our experience that it is possible to understand why the creator did not turn his back on a fallen world. Whilst the Deist view of God[33] as a distant being might be a rational reaction to the presence of evil in the world, it is only when we concede that the God of the bible is not limited by our rational capacities that it becomes possible to begin with the Platonic answer and build upon it. As we do this we see that:

> the way we combine these aspects of God's creative activity has important consequences for the value we set on creation and so for our practical attitudes. If creation is represented as resulting from an almost arbitrary act of will, so that it is a matter of indifference to God whether he creates or refrains from creating, then inevitably the created order is depreciated and deprived of intrinsic value . . . It would be equally mistaken to think that God necessarily creates the world. But if we see creation as proceeding from the loving being of God, and think that creating and sustaining others than himself are actions which accord with and

13

express God's own personal being, this does confer value on the creation and promotes attitudes of caring and responsibility towards it.[34]

We might add that it also suggests that the creation has a future which is locked into the loving purposes of God.

To what extent is God involved within Creation?

From the moment 'God' is linked with the material world it becomes clear that the bible is suggesting that the universe has a personal and divinely rational foundation. Not only does this provide an alternative to the atheistic assumption that the world exists by chance and therefore has no intended destiny[35] but the fact that the two are linked by the word 'create' begs this further question, which again we will look at by examining two competing explanations.

Until comparatively recently the Western Christian understanding about God's relationship with his creation has been dominated by Platonic thought. Under the philosophical tradition of Philo and Aristotle the unity of all reality was broken down into layers. In an attempt to grapple with the multifarious nature of the Greek pantheon of gods it was thought necessary to rank matter into a scale ranging from the highest spiritual realms to the lowest forms of the created order. So, God (or the gods) assumed the pre-eminent position, followed a little lower by the angels, humans, animals, and finally other created matter. Thus the intellectual or the spiritual was thought to be of a far superior order to the merely material; and the task of the spiritual aspirant was to become liberated from every bondage to the material world.

It is said that in this layered view of the world nature became debased since it was thought to have no spiritual value. In fact, since nature was subject to change and decay, and decay was thought to point to imperfection, it was considered *essential* to divorce the divine from the created order because it was simply not possible for the spiritual to associate with ordinary matter. Many commentators believe that this dualistic approach succeeded in cutting humanity off from nature and opened the way for the type of despoliation which has been part of Western culture, certainly since the Industrial Revolution, and possibly longer.[36] This is not to say that the tendencies of the eighteenth century were directly attributable to Plato or Aristotle, but as the age of scientific and technological progress unfolded and it became increasingly possible for humanity to have more of an impact on the environment, their ideas were given a creative expression which was probably far from the philosophers' original intentions. Then later when popular philosophy became dominated by existential thought, nature became humanity's plaything. What is more, the transcendent God of the Platonists easily became Newton's cosmic watchmaker who lived outside the system and allowed it to plot its own course into the future.

This deist world view, in which God is supremely omnipotent but lives in his own cocoon of perfection and is not touched by the world ruled by humans, finds its modern expression in 'secular theology'. In *The Secular City*[37] Harvey Cox describes a world which has become 'disenchanted' of any connection with God and in its secularized state 'neither humanity nor God is defined by his relationship to nature ... [which] ... makes nature itself available for man's use.'[38]

But although Harvey Cox sees the creation as entirely distinct from God, in reality the Hebrew tradition has not even got a word for what we now call 'nature' – meaning non-human self-existent reality. 'It is a concept alien to the Biblical world.'[39] Paulos Mar Gregorios insists that the word for nature (*physis*) is only used in apocryphal works written long after the Old Testament.[40] The fact is that nature was not considered as 'out there' at all, but was welcomed as a gift from God which could not be thought of apart from him. Even in the New Testament, where the word *physis* appears, it is never used to refer to the non-human creation. The view that nature is unimportant is, according to Gregorios, a Greek legacy within Western Christian thought. But such a view of nature has played its part in enabling humanity to act with impunity within the created order, since for so long Christians have been enmeshed within the Greek, rather than Christian, world view. Instead 'the Creator (God of the bible) is not the deist god who makes a machine and the leaves it to operate unaided. Creation continues as a contingent series of endless miracles of his grace.'[41]

Perhaps some strands of Christian thought have never been very successful in replacing the Greek ideas about God and nature with their own because the biblical eschatological hope of a new world order has not been considered to be in keeping with any meaningful attempt to conserve or protect the earth in which we find ourselves. So, if Jesus' teaching that God's redeemed people should be in the world, but not of it[42] leads us to believe that 'the world' *is* inherently evil or unspiritual, it is easy to conclude that God views creation in entirely Platonic terms. The Apostles Paul and John also seem to concur with this understanding when they describe 'the world' as something to be shunned or resisted.[43]

But those who believe that the bible encourages us to think negatively about the created world seem to have misunderstood the intentions of the writers of the New Testament. Whilst it is true that the same Greek word *kosmos* is used in the verses above to describe the world God created; this need not mean that they intend to designate all matter as inherently evil. W.E. Vine shows how the word '*kosmos*' is often used in different ways at different times; and only in a minority of occasions does the context demand that *kosmos* should be interpreted as describing a world that is alienated from and in opposition to God.[44]

In recent years we have seen the emergence of an alternative to the Greek view of nature within Christian thought. This has provided the inspiration for a number of alternative models which attempt to describe God's relationship with his creation. Interestingly, the rise of Liberal Theology seems to have challenged the Greek world view most strongly, since the Greek ideas of a God 'out there' were of no interest to them. 'The Divine' for John Robinson, (quoting Paul Tillich) 'does not inhabit a transcendent world above nature, it is to be found in the "ecstatic" character of this world.'[45]

The result of this thinking was to take away God's watch-maker's eyeglass, and bring him back within the system of creation. But in recent years an earth-centred spirituality has emerged which has embraced the old pagan ideas of pantheism in order to create a god who is not only *within* creation but *is* creation itself. This has provided welcome and fertile soil for ideas like the Gaia Hypothesis,[46] and the theory described in Peter Russell's *The Awakening Earth*[47] which suggests that humans operate collectively like a vast global brain, com-municating alarm, raising consciousness and solving global problems. Russell suggests that this will happen as we undergo a spiritual renewal which will eventually result in 'the progressive integration of human minds into a single living system.'[48]

Another theory which purports to come from within the 'Christian' fold, is the creation-centred spirituality approach, founded by the American Dominican, Matthew Fox. He builds on the work of Teilhard de Chardin, Meister Eckhart and other Christian mystics, and although he retains the use of more of the familiar Christian terminology than they do, his belief that what Christianity needs is a paradigm shift right at its centre means that he is not concerned to retain the traditional definition of the terms he uses. Amongst other things, Fox attacks the traditional Creation/Fall 'ideology' of traditional Christianity, and through the principle of 'interconnectedness' argues that all reality (both spiritual and material) is one. For Fox all kinds of dualism (including the idea of original sin and a transcendent God) are unacceptable, and he prefers the panentheist approach in which all reality is part of God; but God is somehow able to be greater than the sum of his parts. When Fox talks about salvation he insists that it does not come about through overcoming evil or reversing its effects, but through incorporating it with the good into a total unity.[49]

Each of these theories has a certain attractiveness since they are centred around ideas of the oneness of God (if he is acknowledged), mankind and creation. The problem is that none of them squares with the Christian teachings of creation and Fall, and neither do they acknowledge Christ to be of central significance. Whilst the bible does speak of his ongoing relationship with the created order,[50] it never indicates that God *had* to become part of creation in order to relate to it. The pantheistic answer has therefore had a positive impact in so far as it has begun to correct the past over-emphasis on a distant God; which has made humanity largely unconcerned and practically impotent in its care for creation. Its weakness is its resulting over-emphasis upon God's immanence, which has left *him* impotent or unneeded. This has left humans to be their own saviours. Francis Schaeffer criticizes the answers offered by a pantheistic world view for being reductionist, eventually giving no meaning to any of the 'particulars' which together make up the unity of all reality. This, he observes, is not just a philosophical objection. If the only answers we get to the problems of the universe are obtainable from within the system – presumably by projecting our own feelings onto the rest of the created order – we are evading the fact of its separateness and distinctness. What is more, any answers we get by this method fail to satisfy, because we cannot understand why sometimes the nature which is supposed to be part of us is sometimes also an enemy.[51]

The adoption of panentheism[52] by Matthew Fox brings further difficulties.

> The relationship between God and creation which results from this conception of God may be described in dynamic terms as a process of flow and return. Beginning from its enclosure in the divine, creation flows out into multiplicity and returns to unity.[53]

Osborn reflects that what we now call panentheism was traditionally known as emanationism, and is classically reflected in the work of the medieval mystic Hildegard of Bingen.

The factor which separates panentheism from pantheism is the panentheist belief that everything exists *in* God, rather than it being God. This might seem to resonate with the 'In Christ' metaphor Paul uses to denote all that is redeemed by Christ, and may go some way to including the suffering creation within the realm of God's experience without making them one and the same. But the incorporation of a humanity (with freewill and a nature which has its faults) into himself risks implying that there is an imperfection, or even evil, within the nature of God that makes him vulnerable to the point of compromising his sovereignty, and also risks making it impossible for him to deliver the world from evil. So whilst it gets us closer to Paul's assertion that God is 'over all and through all and in all'.[54] I am sure that even panentheism does not go far enough unless it also stresses the 'over all' dimension sufficiently strongly. And it is along these lines that Steve Bishop has reservations about panentheism because he feels that it denies 'creatio ex nihilo'. In panentheism, creation is either presented as 'ex materia'; thus concluding that matter is pre-existent; or it is an emanation from the divine, where 'the divine being's fruitfulness inevitably spills over into a multiplicity of consequences.'[55]

However it is done, the confusion of creator with creation is alien to the biblical perspective.[56] What is more, when Genesis describes the creation of the world it is always clear that God is *distinct* from his handiwork. It is also clear that he did not become subsumed by all that he had made, because he is able to act independently of it and the bible teaches that it fell from fellowship with him without taking him with it.[57] God also sets boundaries for his creation,[58] and talks of becoming its judge and saviour.

It seems that the essential problem with any attempt to construct a model which describes God's relationship with his creation is that each attempt is incomplete when it fails to hold together some of the paradoxical elements within the nature of God. Hugh Montefiore comments:

> No model or analogy can contain God or represent him without distortion. No single model should be given a monopoly, otherwise it almost inevitably ceases to be understood analogically and is understood literally, with the result that its particular distortion is absolutized.[59]

For too long we have been satisfied with incomplete answers to our questions about God and his creation. It is vital that we find correct answers because each incomplete answer leads us further down the road of unwise action. At this point then, it seems sensible to return to the biblical records and see what light they throw on the dilemma.

'God created the Heavens and the Earth'

This very first verse of the bible is special in a number of respects. The first is in its use of the Hebrew word *bara* which is usually rendered 'create'. In each of the forty-eight Old

Testament occurrences the word always has God as the subject, and is only ever used to refer either to his creative activity, or to his saving actions.

> Thus it is apparent that in its theological usage the verb expresses the uniqueness of this work of God as contrasted with man's fashioning and making of various objects out of already existing materials.[60]

At various times the word *bara* has been used to show that Genesis teaches the idea that God created 'out of nothing' (*creatio ex nihilo*), since it never appears with a direct object which would suggest the formation of something new out of something previously in existence, and in the Qal and Niphal stems it never has a human as its subject.[61] The general consensus is that the word *bara* does not always mean 'creation out of nothing' since its use elsewhere does not demand this. Furthermore, John Austin Baker points out that '*creatio ex nihilo*' as a system of thought that 'comes more from later metaphysical understandings of the idea of creation'[62] than out of the plain meaning of the text.[63] But whilst it is true that the *creatio ex nihilo* concept was formalized as a reaction to various heresies in the early church period which insisted that God worked with pre-existent material, it does not follow that it is not present in Genesis 1 since 'verse 1 stands with good reason before verse 2'.[64]

The idea of creation from nothing is more explicitly stated in the New Testament where its various writers include phrases which 'show that creation involves the beginning of the existence of the world, so that there is no pre-existent matter.'[65] So when Paul says that God 'calls into existence the things that do not exist' (Romans: 4:17) and that he commanded light to shine out of darkness (2 Corinthians: 4:6), he is probably suggesting that the event occurred without any prior material cause – especially since when *ktizo* (create) is used elsewhere in

Greek it describes the founding of a city, house or colony that previously did not exist.[66] The writer to the Hebrews supports this when he states that 'the universe was formed at God's command, so that what is seen was not made out of what was visible'[67] – implying a belief that 'there was no material involved in bringing into being the whole of the reality about us.'[68]

In any case the debate only applies to one verse. When we encounter the idea again in Genesis verses 1:21 and 27 and 5:1-2, it is clear that these subsequent creative acts presuppose an already created (although formless) earth. Albert Wolters comments:

> We cannot strictly speak of 'creatio ex nihilo' in the case of God's creative fiats in the six days. Instead, creation here has the character of elaborating and completing the unformed state of reality.[69]

Wolters uses the term *creatio prima* to describe the primordial creation out of nothing (his *creatio ex nihilo*) and adopts the phrase *creatio secunda* to refer to all God's work of elaboration and completion of creation after this first verse. Between them, these two distinct moments of God's creation are presented as all-encompassing. Thus it is not possible to attribute any part of creation to any other deity or material cause. Both the phrase 'the Heavens and the Earth' in Genesis 1:1, and the Greek phrase *ta panta* (all things) emphasize this point.[70]

Despite the significance of the *'creatio ex nihilo'* concept, James Houston believes that it is potentially misleading if too great an emphasis is placed upon it. This is because it inevitably turns the attention to speculation about *how* the universe was formed and the nature of the nothingness which 'preceded' it.[71] Houston prefers to focus his attention upon what he believes to be a consistently biblical theme. namely *'Creatio per Verbum'*. For Houston it is the call of God that is significant since it is the Word of God which determines what is to be. 'Each deed of creation is accomplished by the Word. God's will is spoken, and with His speech the deed is done. The Word is the deed.'[72]

Houston believes that the way the Hebrew word *amar* (God's creative Word[73]) is used in Genesis 1 emphasizes the pledge of God to sustain what he has brought into being. So each command is also God's provision for creation, since he never commands where he does not also provide for the command's fulfillment. Thus, in Houston's account, it is God's intention that all things actualize their potential with everything pointing 'beyond itself to a directed end, from which all the processes receive their meaning and purpose, in a miraculous unfolding of coherence in all things.'[74] So even when God causes The Word to become flesh,[75] it is clear that he is still engaged in the task of realizing his vision for creation.

The fact that Genesis 1.1 begins as it does is significant in so far as it suggests that in the very first verse a foundational point is being made. The very words 'in the beginning' imply that the writer intends us to assume that nothing existed until this moment except God in all his fullness.[76] This assurance that God created all things[77] from the beginning of time also keys into another concept familiar to the Hebrews, and referred to in Isaiah 46:10, namely that the God who is the beginning and the end also has a purpose for all that he created. This idea of purpose is underlined by the use of the Hebrew word *yatsar* in 2:7, 8 and 19. *Yatsar* conjures up images of God lovingly fashioning according to a specific design for a predetermined purpose.[78]

Alongside the word *bara*, there is another word in Chapter 1 which merits attention at this point. The Hebrew word *asa* is translated 'made' in verses 7, 16 and 25; and many commentators think it is used alongside *bara* for a very good reason. Francis Schaeffer believes that it is used in order to

23

highlight the more special word *bara*, which marks three distinct points in the creation story. The first time *bara* occurs is the point at which God created matter out of nothing (Gen. 1:1); the second time it describes the creation of conscious life (Gen. 1:21), and the final occasion marks the entry of humanity (used 3 times – Gen. 1:27).

The point here is not so much that *bara* is used to indicate a particular way of creating, but that in parallel with *asa* the two cover the whole range of the creator's work. The use of the two together is the writer's way of highlighting the special by placing it alongside the usual. Schaeffer then turns to Genesis 5:1-2; which repeats the thrust of 1:27; again using the word *bara* three times. It is the triple emphasis here which Schaeffer believes is especially worthy of note, indicating that the author is saying something which is in need of even greater emphasis.

We conclude from all this that it is wrong to see the creation story as having just one climax – the creation of humans in 1:26. Certainly, each occurrence of *bara* builds on the last and its triple emphasis in 1:27 indicates this verse as the highest of high points, but the whole of creation is all of a piece.

'And the Spirit of God was hovering over the waters'

This pregnant phrase speaks of the intimacy and creativity of God's continuing relationship with his creation. Not only did God choose to create but his Spirit – the Old Testament term for the outpouring of God's creative energy – is described as hovering over the face of the earth. This same term reappears in Deuteronomy 32:11 when it describes the mother eagle stirring its young into flight. Kidner says that this picture of intimacy and contact must be kept in mind throughout.[79] Jürgen Moltmann attributes a great deal to the presence of the Spirit here since he is convinced that 'in the gift and through the powers of the Holy Spirit a new divine presence is experienced in creation.'[80] This is perhaps the ultimate indication that the creation is the work of a God who is still creating, and who has further plans for the future.

'God separated the light from the darkness'

Claus Westermann sees emphasis as being tremendously significant in this passage[81] and notes that the first three acts of creation each involve an act of separation; followed by the naming of day and night, the sky, the land and the seas. It is the story of the separation and naming of each part of the creation which is illustrative of an inherent order within creation. Francis Schaeffer sees the Genesis story as giving us a picture of creation perfectly at peace with itself – the *shalom* motif of peace, pointing to a complete unity with a history which was proceeding towards its God intended goal.[82] Tim Marks notes how *shalom* implies good order and fullness, implying health and well-being.[83]

'God called . . .'

The process of naming is also important in the Hebrew world since it meant more than simply attaching a label of identification, but indicated that the one doing the naming had a deep knowledge of that being named and therefore had a sympathetic relationship with it.[84] God therefore names only those things which are the result of his own creative activity. Westermann says:

> by naming them, God destines space and time to be the world of humanity for ever, and in this same action shows himself to be the master so defined . . . Talk about the creator therefore is talk about the master of creation.[85]

This leaves Adam the space to define his more immediate and personal surroundings himself, whilst providing that given framework which reminds him who is the Lord over creation.

So far then we have seen that a biblical view of nature begins with an understanding of God's relationship with it as described in the early chapters of Genesis. I have suggested that it teaches us that God is the maker of all things; and he is not to be confused with what he has created, for he does not depend on it but sustains it himself. The distinctness of God from his creation need not imply disinterest as the Greeks and secular theologians supposed, and as humans throughout the ages have suggested by their actions. In fact any impression of aloofness or detachment is contradicted by the presence of God's Spirit at the beginning, and throughout the history of the world. God is thus able to be lovingly involved with his creation precisely *because* he is also separate from it. So he can be perfectly loving towards it and involved within it through his Spirit, and at the same time is able to give himself for his creation because he also exists outside it. Therefore the immanence of God is, in a sense, dependent upon his otherness because only a God who also exists outside creation is able to bring into being everything he wishes for it. The bible also teaches us that the creation is not inherently evil (as dualist religions might suppose) or a product of chance; but it is intrinsically good (although fallen) and cared for by God.

'Let the land produce living creatures'

Jeanne Kay replaces the Greek hierarchical view of creation with what she describes as a biblical view in which both living nature and humanity occupy the same intermediate level of being somewhere between God and potter's clay. So although English translations of verses 24-6 interpret *nefesh chayah* as 'creatures', she points out that the same Hebrew words are used elsewhere to refer to the human soul.[86] What is more, the word *ruach*, variously translated as spirit or breath, is the same life-force with which God animates *all* life. So in the following verses from Ecclesiastes 3 the italicized words are all translations of *ruach*:

Man's fate is like that of the animals; the same fate awaits them both. As one dies, so dies the other. All have the same *breath* . . . Who knows if the *spirit* of man rises upward and if the *spirit* of the animal goes down into the earth?[87]

Kay concludes:

This use of the same terms for both human and animal souls, combined with our joint creation on the sixth day, suggests more similarities in biblical human and animal conditions than is generally recognized.[88]

And this is not surprising since it is from the earth that both man and creatures are made.[89] As George Caird comments: 'While God is spirit, man, like the beasts, is flesh, and the flesh constitutes a bond of union with the whole animal kingdom.'[90]

'And God saw that it was good . . . It was very good'

The theme of goodness runs like a golden thread throughout the creation story, and on through the whole of scripture. This is not simply because the word 'good' is repeated seven times in one chapter (although this itself is worthy of note) but also because the goodness of creation unfolds into the covenant of intended blessing for the whole earth (see Genesis 12:2-3) and ultimately on into the 'good news' of salvation brought by God's son. Thus 'the creation of a good world is the backdrop against which the drama of Old Testament history takes place.'[91]

Creation and salvation are therefore to be seen as inter-related themes, for:

the Doctrine of creation, as developed in the Old Testament, is all about humanity's relationship with the rest of the created order. This is why it must be a starting point for Christians to think about how they should respond to modern environmental issues.[92]

The depth and breadth of the word 'good' indicates that exegetes who have understood it as describing its usefulness to the yet-to-be-created human beings have not gone far enough. Goodness implies that creation has value, and from this we can derive a number of important points.

The first is that a good creation is an inherently beautiful creation. Claus Westermann argues that in the Old Testament the word 'beautiful' describes an event rather than a being.[93] Thus it is the encounter, and the experience of that encounter which is described as beautiful. To the Hebrew mind the presence of beauty was to be celebrated rather than simply contemplated or judged. It has an indefinable quality. This explains the existence of the psalms of praise, because it is in praise that the beauty of creation is grasped, and we might add that it is through attempts to define and categorize the experience that its beauty is sometimes lost.

Secondly goodness also relates to diversity and interdependence. So, it is a recognition of the diversity of creation that leads Job[94] and the Psalmist[95] to silence and praise respectively; illustrating the wonder and praise evoked within the heart of humanity when confronted with the true reality of all God has made. The earth is therefore good because, despite the ravages of humanity, it retains its capacity to amaze all who study it.

So far we have only approached the goodness of creation from a human standpoint; but Genesis 1 presents us with God's judgements, not ours. This, according to Westermann, must also mean that creation is good for that which God intends it,[96] and that it has a certain value given to it by virtue of the fact that it is created by God. Thus this judgement is not diminished because in our experience there is evil as well as good in creation, for the negative experiences point to a different issue which we will deal with later. The goodness of creation is a given quality which is present because creation still has a purpose, no matter how thwarted and distorted by sin, and also has a destiny[97] because it has not been cast off by its creator. The Heavens and Earth are good because they bring joy to God. This is most clearly seen in Genesis 1:31-2:3 when God completes his work and takes his rest of achievement. There is praise and delight at the completing of the task which is expressed in the final evaluation 'It is very good'. It is as though each constituent part is good, but the whole is perfect because it finally speaks to the glory of its creator and lives as a permanent revelation of him – even in its fallen state.[98] In this context it seems wrong to make too much of the distinction Christian theologians sometimes make between 'natural' revelation and 'specific' revelation[99] as if the former were vastly inferior and superseded now we have the latter. Paul confirms this when he proclaims the glory of creation even in its fallen state; and affirms its ability to point humanity to God.[100] It also lifts the concept of goodness above the merely 'useful' and into the realm of that which is essentially good whether or not humanity views it as such.

The way we treat nature depends, rather obviously, on our understanding of its value and worth. For men and women with no belief in God as the creator of all things (or no understanding of what a faith in a 'creator' implies) that worth will often be measured in terms of the benefit they (or others) derive from it. Its value may therefore be quantified in economic terms[101] or by using some other, less well defined measure such as its usefulness to society or its symbolic value. The important thing to recognize here is that any value assigned using these criteria is unashamedly utilitarian – and only measures value from a human perspective.[102]

For Christians, who have a belief in God as the creator of all things, the route to determining the value of our gift and inheritance is rather different since we recognize that creation has an inherent value given to it by God. When it comes to

29

assigning a value to nature, Christian theology has commonly taken one of two avenues. The first is inherited from Plato, and insists that creation can be ordered, and non-human creation be labelled 'nature' and treated as 'of third order value'[103] existing simply as proof that there is a creator. Within Platonic thought the highest value is therefore largely confined within a human-God axis, where God is solely interested in saving humanity from the consequences and punishment brought about by *his* sin; and delivering him from his bondage to this material world. Such an understanding does not value nature, except in as far as it serves to meet our needs and desires, and has little idea or concern about how it relates to God.

The second route is taken by the pantheists and panentheists for whom all of nature has value because it is *part of* God himself. They switch the focus of attention from humanity to the universe in which we are merely one participant amongst many. This tries to solve the problem of alienation between God, humanity and creation by wrapping them all up into one package. In the light of the texts we have examined, neither of these is any longer found to be sufficient.

This is currently significant where secular environmental ethicists are struggling with the concept of giving 'intrisic value' to species, landscapes etc. in order to build sound arguments for their preservation. Vacuous philosophical questions like the conundrum 'If a tree falls in the forest and no one is there to hear it, does it make a sound' illustrate the anthropocentric direction of human thinking where there is no adequate reason to assign such value to creation.

It is the very fact that God reached out from beyond himself and created a world which not only exists but which flourishes and develops that is the Christian's answer to this problem of assigning value. The way the story develops is also a sign that the creator wishes to continue to reveal himself to mankind. George Hendry believes that it also indicates that God's desire is to continue to bless that which he has created.[104] Creation then is a revelation of God's faithfulness and love as well as his goodness and glory. So the very creator who made the world and declared it to be good also sustains his creation in order that it should continue to declare his nature to the whole of fallen mankind.

'Then God said. "Let us make humans in our image"'

The magical expression 'create' is finally used to describe what many view to be the pinnacle of God's creative act, the creation of mankind. Whilst it is true that 'all things are equal in their origin, as far as creation is concerned,'[105] humanity has a special nature which is given by God. it is men and women alone which bear the *image* of their creator. The whole of the next chapter will be devoted to this subject, but for now we record the words of Jürgen Moltmann.

> As God's work, creation is not essentially similar to the creator; it is the expression of his will. But as image, men and women correspond to the creator in their very essence, because in these created beings God corresponds to himself. It is here that the supreme analogy in creation is created . . . As God's image, men and women are beings who correspond to God . . . In a certain sense God enters into the creatures whom he has designated to be his image.[106]

'I give you every seed bearing plant . . . for food'

Although God gave humanity the task of ruling over all the earth, including its creatures, only the seed-bearing plants were given them for food. To put it plainly – God gave plants for animals to eat. John Cobb Jr. suggests that this implies a non-symmetrical relation within the divine order of things.[107] If humans have been permitted to eat plants but not animals, their relationship with each must be intrinsically different – implying that we also have a different responsibility for each.

31

Here in Genesis 1 humans are prohibited to shed any blood, but are allowed to eat plants; whereas in Genesis 9 we read the post-Fall command which supersedes this chapter and which takes account of the Fall and the changes that brings. In chapter 9 humans are allowed to eat animals – subject to certain restrictions – but are still to regard the taking of human life as forbidden. We will consider the meaning of this change in Chapter Two, but for now we note that both these verses imply 'that there are grades of value and diversities of rights.'[108]

There are many who would profoundly disagree with this point, believing it to be the thin end of the wedge of human centredness. But this need only be the case if it is humanity who retains the authority to determine the criteria we use to assign value. Just because I suggest that this passage indicates that plants are not as important as animals, and animals are not as important as humans does not mean that either plants or animals are unimportant. This will become clearer as my argument unfolds. It is in fact those who try to insist that *all* life is sacrosanct who make it harder for humanity to live with the belief that non-human life has an inherent value. If it all has equal value it would be impossible to step on the ground, let alone live in praise of the creator. In practice we all live with this differentiated value concept firmly embedded in our beings – for if we did not, we would soon starve to death.

Conclusion: The Meaning of Creation
Each discovery we make about the fabric and design of our planet illustrates to us that all God's handiwork bears a certain hallmark of its creator. What is more, we are able to understand God's revelation because we too are part of God's creation and there is a correspondence between the rational minds of human beings and the rational order of the physical world.

For those Christians who incorporate the ideas of Plato into the teaching of the bible, the logical reaction would range from an otherworldly disregard for the state of the environment (and for some the thinning ozone layer or rapid species loss might even be a welcome sign that this earth is coming to its conclusion, and the return of Christ is therefore imminent) to a concern about issues of conservation but only in as far as they relate to human self-interest. This reflects their view that nature has little value.

For those with pantheist ideas about God, the problems are real, but humans are thought of as their own ecological saviours because God is leading the world to greater wholeness by uniting its elements. Since God is thought to be an evolving deity at the heart of the universe who is constantly experimenting and restoring vital equilibria, salvation (such as it is) is either attained by natural planetary evolution (Gaia) or is reached as humans harness the power God has given them (through science and technology) and work with the pattern of the universe.

What I have sought to do thus far is to show that there are flaws in both these 'extremes' since they fail to take proper account of the biblical doctrine of creation. The bible neither teaches a structured 'Greek style' universe, or a reductionist view of creation. As Richard Russell says: 'the biblical view rejects the idea that man exists for nature or nature exists for man.'[109]

I hope I have been able to demonstrate that a truly biblical Christian theology teaches that both humanity and nature exist for the glory and purposes of God who is Lord over *and* sustainer of all things. Thus it is the biblical view of nature that gives it value in itself, and which gives humanity the dignity and value we deserve as a special part of nature. Both the Platonic and pantheistic views fall short, because in different ways they make humanity and nature autonomous from their creator. The Platonist implies that God has devolved responsibility for the creation to humanity and is relatively unconcerned about it; and the pantheist believes that God and nature are one, and by discovery of this inter-relatedness we can discover the path to unity and wholeness. In practice, both fail to appreciate that God is both within *and* above creation and has laid down any absolute guidelines whereby God and humanity can together govern creation in a godly manner.

Now it is quite obvious that Christendom does not split itself neatly into card-carrying Platonists on one hand, and avowed pantheists on the other. By far the most common Christian understanding of God's relationship with his creation is the one I have been arguing for: namely the theistic position which attempts to hold God's transcendence and immanence together in a sort of harmony.

Lynn White criticized Christian theology for overthrowing pagan attitudes of reverence for nature and introducing a domineering religion which had no respect for nature.[110] What I hope I have been able to illustrate is that true Christian theology teaches no such thing. I hope I have also made it clear that the Genesis story indicates that neither of these two views about nature are biblically faithful as they stand. The biblical records teach that nature bears the imprint of the creator and is separate from him but sacred. This sacredness demands our reverence of nature but forbids its worship since it is only created. God respects and values *all* that he created and expects human beings to do the same, recognizing that in the economy of God the future of humanity and the future of the earth are bound up together.

> Nature imposes values because it is creation . . . The biblical tradition offers us a picture of a world which has taken reverence for life seriously and which is therefore transparent to the deeper goodness of all creation.[111]

The Creation of Humanity

At the centre of the creation story is the creator; with all he has created existing as a hymn of praise to him, and as a tribute to his wisdom and power. Moltmann believes that this essential unity of all things puts the creation of humanity into perspective.[112] God will reveal that humanity indeed has a special place in the creator's scheme, but we are also part of the creation which together points upwards towards God. This said, in this section I want to focus attention upon humanity and what we were created to be. Before I consider the biblical texts it will first be helpful to recognize the other traditions of thought which prevail today.

What is Human?

There are two main non-biblical views about human nature. The predominant view comes, again, from Platonic roots. This view was born and refined during the period 100 BC-AD 200 and therefore influenced the early Christian theologians. We have already seen that Plato taught that reality was made up of two parts; the material realm which is imperfect; and the spiritual realm which is the world of ideas, and is more perfect than the first because it is permanent. In early Platonic thought the gods also occupied this spiritual realm, but this idea became refined as, under the influence of Christian thought, 'the gods' became 'one supreme transcendent Mind' who was at the head of the hierarchy of beings. The human soul also occupied the spiritual realm, but it became fallen and lay trapped in the material body longing for release.

The purpose of life was therefore to purify the soul by philosophy (which is derived from the supreme mind) so that it might return to a disembodied existence in which it could once again enjoy the vision of true reality. Neo-platonists further refined these ideas and taught that a human possessed a 'higher' and a 'lower' soul. The higher soul is in contact with the spiritual realm, whereas the lower soul can only remain in touch with the body. It is therefore the higher soul which can achieve release by contemplating detachment from bodily desires, and the lower or bodily part of humanity is of negative value. Thus Platonists have, at various times, believed that the body can either be despised or indulged to no spiritual detriment.

The second view has its roots firmly within the Western materialistic culture, and it largely ignores the existence of any spiritual realm altogether. Thus humans are somewhat deterministically described as the product of matter plus time plus chance. This is seen in action in a number of different systems: for example, Karl Marx believed that humans were the product of scientific laws of history and are controlled by economic forces; Sigmund Freud looked to early life experiences and believed that they shaped the sub-conscious mind, which in turn affected human behaviour; and B.F. Skinner propounded behaviourist theories in which human behaviour is simply the product of either immediate or inherited environmental factors. These are but three examples of a widely influential genre.

So in the materialistic view, the value of the human being is derived primarily from our conformity to given norms and the resulting contribution to wider society. Each of these views also has its own definitions of the means to salvation: control over the means of production; psycho-analysis; and behavioural conditioning. At the root of all of them is the need to improve an imperfect environment which produces imperfect people.

Turning again to the bible, James Houston reminds us that 'the true humanity of man is dependent upon God, not man.'[113] This reminds us that the Christian view of humanity begins with one simple confession: that we are all *created* beings, who in common with the rest of creation were created to be dependent upon God and enjoy a relationship with him.

Thus in our physical nature we are like non-human creatures since we are made of the same stuff by the same creator. And yet, as we saw at the end of the last section, we are also different by virtue of the fact that unlike them we have been created in the image of God. In order to understand the uniqueness of humanity and its resultant impact upon the rest of the created order we therefore need to look at what this phrase means.

'So God created mankind in his own image'

Attempts to picture the pre-Fall state of humanity have always been fraught with difficulty because we are dealing with such a small amount of biblical material. What is more, assumptions such as the suggestion that pre-Fall creation can be equated with the visions of redeemed creation in Isaiah and Revelation are intriguing but tenuous and impossible to prove. The best hope we have of discovering the nature and purpose of ideal humanity seems to lie in this phrase 'in his own image.'

Genesis 1:26-28 is possibly the most discussed passage in the whole of the creation story. We have already looked at the meaning of the word *bara* earlier, and we noted that the triple emphasis on that word indicates that this is a high point in the account. The first thing to notice is that if we are prepared to accept that men and women together constitute 'humankind' and so together are made in God's image, the image of God metaphor also receives triple emphasis in these verses. The importance of this phrase is also matched by its usefulness, for in this section in which we have set out to discover what humanity was created to *be* as opposed to what we *became*, it is this phrase which offers us most of the clues. Indeed as far as the Old Testament is concerned, 'the image of God is what makes man man.'[114] The meaning of the phrase has usually been understood in one of three ways.

I) The Substantive View

This is what might be termed the traditional view, and was held by many theologians until the time of the Reformation. It seems to have been based upon early attempts to define the Hebrew word *tselem* (image). In some places in the Old Testament the word is used to refer to the kind of statue or idol erected by Israel's neighbours.[115] It is not hard to see how from the translation 'statue' the idea grew up that humanity was created in order to physically resemble God. The traditional translation 'according to his image' used in Genesis 1:26-28 has also unwittingly played its part in perpetuating this confusion. This most literal understanding of the concept of the image has never been very widespread, but has a long history amongst various heretical groups and in current times the Mormons teach similar ideas.

In most places *tselem* is not used to mean a physical image. This has encouraged some to assume that human possession of the image means that we describe God in a metaphorical sense. Thus, for example, the fact that men and women walk upright is thought to be the creator's way of reminding us that God is a morally upright deity. Other substantive views have suggested that the image is expressed in more spiritual ways; most commonly by the exercise of the human power of reason. This, not surprisingly, came from within Greek thought, which commonly supposed that the most important feature of humanity was our capacity for rational thought: (*homo sapiens* = the thinking being). However the Greeks were not always in agreement as to how to define reason. Plato believed that the highest exercising of the human capacity of reason was seen as he engaged in contemplative thought; whereas Aristotle (and later Aquinas) favoured its more empirical forms which led to scientific discovery and thus helped mankind exercise control. Whatever the definition of reason, the implication of the substantive view was that, since humanity 'possessed' the power of reason 'by nature', it was God's way of indicating that he had given human beings a power which was intended to ensure that we could make our own way in the world; and that as we grew in mental stature, greater control and domination by the human race over nature would eventually follow. The idea that the limits of our activities were only determined by our inventiveness, so that 'what becomes humanly possible' is 'what should be', is in keeping with the Greek view of a wholly transcendent deity.

The Platonic emphasis upon reason as the content of the image was encouraged by verses in the New Testament such as Colossians 3:10[116] which seemed to indicate that the image of God contained at least some kind of intellectual endowment; and by the fact that the ability to think and plan rationally in order to exercise control does seem to be one of the most striking differences between humanity and the rest of the animal kingdom.

Those who held to the substantive view in the early centuries tended to distinguish between the words image (*tselem*) and likeness (*demut*) in Genesis 1:26-28. In the light of Genesis 5:1-3; 9:5-6; 1 Corinthians 11:7 and James 3:9, Irenaeus argued that humanity was created in God's image, but only gradually evolved into his likeness as God's spirit endowed him with it as a gift of God's grace.[117] Thomas Aquinas then insisted that human reason existed within the 'image' part of humanity and therefore resided permanently (and in an unfallen state) within every person.[118] During medieval times this was developed further, with the idea that the 'likeness' contained the moral attributes of God which had to be relearned after the Fall; and the 'image' embraced God's natural attributes (most notably reason and knowledge) which were still available to humanity in an untouched form.

The Reformation brought a change in thinking, as both Luther and Calvin rejected the distinction between the image and the likeness of God on the grounds that Genesis 1:26 is typical Hebrew parallelism and that the two terms therefore refer to the same thing, not two different things. The point they wished to make was that the image of God should be equated with original (pre-Fall) righteousness, and that in fallen humans it remains a potentiality (Luther) or a relic (Calvin).

II) The Relational View
The idea that the image of God resides within humanity is most strongly challenged by Emil Brunner and Karl Barth. For Brunner, it is the Word of God which constitutes the image of God and so it is only possible to understand our own nature fully when we are in a full relationship with God through Jesus (the living Word of God). Brunner makes a distinction between what he calls the 'formal' image of God – that which makes a person human as opposed to an animal and is untouched by the Fall; and the 'material' image – which recognizes that God did not make men and women in a finished state as he did the other animals, but created within them the potentiality to realize the implications of being human.[119] Although at first sight this appears to be similar to Irenaeus and Aquinas, Brunner insists that this view is not substantive but relational. This is because humanity has been given the opportunity to respond to God by virtue of the formal image which is within him, but it is only as he makes a response to God that the material image is present. Thus in our humanity we stand before God and are responsible to him whether we recognize it or not. So each person is always in relationship with God, but is only able to realize the potential of being in his image (and therefore fully human) when he makes a response to God's invitation.

Karl Barth saw things a little differently, preferring to believe that humans are only in relationship with God after conversion, and thus he sees the image of God as our *potentiality* for relationship.[120] According to Barth, humanity is a replication of God who created from within a Trinitarian relationship ('Let *us* create'). So God gives humanity the most natural means to express our given capacity for relationship when he decides that the race should consist of both male and female who, by virtue of design, are created for a complementary relationship with each other.[121] This social nature of humans therefore reflects the nature of God as a community of persons existing in a love relationship. The image of God in humans is then seen as grounded in their existence in a relationship of responsibility to God. In the state of original righteousness this relationship is marked by love, trust and obedience. For fallen humans it is a relationship of rebellion and disobedience – but it is still a relationship of responsibility to God which marks us off from the animals. In Christ the state of 'original righteousness' is restored.

Barth believed that we learn most about humanity not by studying ourselves but by looking at Jesus. So for a picture of how this relational aspect of our character is ideally worked out in practice we need go no further than look at the life of Jesus. the perfect man, the possessor of the unfallen image of God, and his fully revealed Word. As we look at Jesus we see that he had a perfect relationship with his Father[122] whilst also being united with him in purpose[123] and showing compassion and forgiveness for the human race which was alienated from such perfect fellowship.[124] If Jesus was fully human then Barth contends that this set of inter-relationships is the God given manifestation of complete humanity.

III) The Functional View

This view is most similar to the relational, since proponents of it contend that the image of God is not something that is present within humanity but the image is seen as it is worked out in practice. The function most frequently connected to the image of God within the functional view is the exercising of human dominion over the earth. This is because in Genesis 1:26-28 the themes of the image of God and dominion are linked twice in a way which is thought to be more than coincidental. It is argued that this same connection between the themes is also seen in Psalm 8:5-6, with verse 5 thought to be a natural equivalent to the image of God metaphor in Genesis. Leonard Verduin says:

> Again the idea of dominion-having stands out as the central feature. That man is a creature meant for dominion-having and that as such he is in the image of his maker – this is the burden of the creation account given in Genesis.[125]

The Meaning of 'The Image of God'

Having briefly observed the three main views on the image of God, I now want to evaluate them and examine the implications of each to our theology of the environment.

The first thing I want to do is to affirm two important foundational points. The first is that the image of God is universal within the human race. It is Adam (the universal man) who is made in the image of God, and the bible clearly suggests that we have inherited this image.[126] At the time this section of Genesis was written the idea of the image of God was not new, but it was more usually applied to Kings and Pharaohs.[127] Thus the application of the image to *all* men and women is strikingly important. The second point which needs stressing is that the bible teaches that the image of God has not been lost as a result of the Fall, although it is affected by it.[128] References to it after Genesis 3 clearly presuppose this. We can therefore assume from these two points that the image is not something which is given by God as a reward for correct behaviour or as a sign of a special relationship only available to a few. The image of God is possessed by all humans in equal measure, and therefore is to be understood as something which is part of our essential humanity. This affirms our special place in creation and also suggests that we have a unique destiny.

Given the above, the first conclusion we should make is that the image of God is primarily substantive because it relates to our essential makeup. We have a certain ability to produce art, to appreciate aesthetic beauty and to order our lives that animals do not possess to the same degree. But the substantive view does not provide the complete answer since the choice of reason above all other human attributes reflects Greek obsessions, not biblical teaching. If reason were to *be* the image it would also suggest that some people possess it more than others. In fact, the particular quality of reason is better seen as existing as a *result* of possessing the image rather than being the image of God itself.

To choose to elevate reason above all other divine and human attributes could be seen as an attempt to try and make God into our image, since it is based upon our own hierarchical order of merit. It is not surprising that it was welcomed by theologians, since they represent the branch of Christendom which would most naturally be elevated above the rest. It has also been convenient to place such importance upon reason, for in doing so it has been possible for us to believe we exist within a dualistic universe in which we can do what we like with the natural order and God shows no concern. We should also mention here that the early Greek understanding of Genesis 1:26-28 is also not favoured by most modern scholars. They agree with Luther and Calvin that there is no justification for reading a distinction between 'image' and 'likeness' into the passage. Thus this limited view of humanity has, in practice, only succeeded in ministering to our belief in our own supremacy, and in doing so we have fallen into the same trap as Adam and Eve did in the garden. It has helped us believe that it is by asserting our independence that we can grow and

achieve our full potential, and that God has sanctioned whatever behaviour we deem necessary to achieve our own ends.[129]

So although I am suggesting that the image of God has a
substantive foundation, I do not believe that the substantive
model is the complete answer. Up to this point I have suggested
that the major weaknesses of the other two views are found in
the fact that they seem to have isolated *consequences* of being in
the image of God and put the proverbial cart before the horse
by suggesting that they *are* the image. The very nature of a
metaphor demands that we understand that it cannot ever
fully describe its object;[130] and when we understand that the
image of God metaphor cannot be tied down by one
description it frees us to be able to look at the other two
suggestions in order to try and use whatever light they shed on
our understanding of the image.

When Henri Blocher makes the point that *tselem* does not
speak primarily about the nature of the human creature, but
about his constitutive relationships he is describing how
humans are the 'created representation of their creator'[131] and
the image of God's own glory.[132] This gives new meaning to the
prohibition of the making of godlike images.[133] What God is
saying is that he has already placed his image into the world in
the form of men and women. His expectation is that each
person will pay due respect to that image by treating himself
and his fellow human beings correctly and by giving to God
what is his.[134] It is hardly surprising then that in Colossians 3,
in which the image of God metaphor is picked up in the
context of its being renewed in Christ, Paul tells the Christians
in Colossae not to carry on defiling the image in themselves by
dishonouring their bodies or in other people by engaging in
slanderous behaviour.[135] This application of the image of God
idea also resonates with the 'greatest commandments'[136] and
other New Testament writings.[137]

The meaning of the image of God metaphor is perhaps

further clarified by reference to Genesis 5:3. After restating that humanity is created in God's image, the writer describes Adam's son Seth as being in his father's image. The writer of Genesis is clearly trying to make an important point by juxtaposing these two uses of the image metaphor. God is indicating that he views humanity to be in similar relationship with him as Adam was with Seth. Thus this passage shows that God is declaring that he created mankind to be earthly representations of his own being who are also capable of response and relationship. This is supported by the New Testament where Luke calls Adam the son of God[138] and in Acts says 'we are his [God's] offspring.'[139] Henri Blocher suggests that this idea is not stressed more strongly in Genesis in order to avoid pantheistic confusion at a time when ideas that humans were divine were common misconceptions. It is not until the New Testament that ordinary individuals are derivatively, and therefore safely, referred to as being, by adoption, the sons of God. Jürgen Moltmann says:

> Human likeness to God consists in the fact that human beings, for their part, correspond to God. The God who allows his Glory to light up his image on earth and so shine forth from that image, is reflected in human beings as in a mirror.[140]

Claus Westermann warns against dethroning the image metaphor from its place at the centre of our understanding of ourselves when in answer to the question 'What does the phrase mean?' he says:

> It is not a declaration about man, but about the creation of man. The meaning can only be understood from what has preceded the creative act. The text is making a statement about an action of God who decides to create man in his image. The meaning must come from the creation event.[141]

From the beginning of Christian history, theologians have studied the symbol with a view to gaining a greater understanding about ourselves and our inherent qualities. Westermann reminds us that at the centre of the symbol is God. It was God who resolved to create us, and who exhorted himself to implant his own image within each person.[142]

It is only when we begin from this place that we can place humanity in correct perspective to the world in which he lives. In a subsection of his book, entitled 'Facts of Relationship',[143] Rowland Moss sets out the special ways in which humanity excels over the animals in a section entitled 'Man as distinct from the rest of nature'. It covers many of the points we have just considered and more we will come to later. But this section is quite correctly placed next to another entitled 'Man as an integral part of nature.' Within this section he considers Genesis 1:31 in which God expresses his delight at the completed creation, and notes that it makes no distinction between the creation of humanity and the fruits of his previous five days of activity. Douglas John Hall indicates how this one verse is in fact more in keeping with chapter 2[144] since the second chapter generally emphasizes our 'affinity with the dust' whereas chapter 1 mostly prefers to major on our distinction from the basic 'stuff of creation.'[145] We are made in God's image but also share the garden and the Sabbath day with the other creatures, are made of the same dust as them,[146] feed as they feed[147] and are similarly blessed in their reproduction.[148] It is as we appreciate our natural connectedness with the rest of creation, that we also begin to see where the human roots of our desire to care for creation begin.

As we move away from the obsession with equating the image with some inherent human quality it becomes possible to examine the part relationship might play in our essential humanity. God created the human being to correspond to himself, and since he exists in relationship (within the Trinity) so mankind is only truly human as he is also within relationships. Jürgen Moltmann agrees with Calvin and Luther that it is wrong to read a doctrine of the Trinity into the Genesis text, and yet he insists that this passage helps us understand the God who is Triune. He then says.

> Whereas a self-resolving God is a plural in the singular, his image on earth – the human being – is apparently supposed to be singular in the plural. The one God, who is differentiated in himself and is one with himself, then finds his correspondence in a community of human beings, female and male, who unite with one another and are one.[149]

This leads us to an appreciation of the fact that:

> What God has decided to create must stand in a relationship to him. The creation of man in God's image is directed to something happening between God and man. The creator created a creature that corresponds to him, to whom he can speak, and who can hear him.[150]

'It belongs to the biblical tradition that the human creature is to be understood within the context of its manifold relatedness.'[151] So although we cannot directly correlate the image of God with the capacity for relationships or make it dependent upon the exercise of dominion, both of these ideas open the way for an appreciation that God created human beings for a purpose which preceded the Fall and was, in some way, not thwarted by it. Thus God's intention for us was that we know, love and obey him as creator and sustainer, and steward the creation wisely under his direction. We were also intended to exercise dominion over the rest of the created order. The result of being created in the image of God then is that humanity is able to reflect those Godly qualities which, when fully reflected in men and women in right relationship with the creator make the fulfilment of our destiny possible, and help us to see that in doing this correctly we are playing a part in fulfilling the God-ordained destiny for the rest of the planet.

Conclusion: The Nature of Humanity

I conclude that none of the three models which purport to understand and explain the meaning and implications of mankind created in the image of God are complete in themselves. Thus although the image is primarily a substantive *concept*, the 'substantive model' fails to take full account of the implications of mankind being made in God's image. It also appears to be too human centred, because when it states that humanity is the high point of creation it fails to notice that whilst he was the last created being, the sixth day was not the end of the week for the creator. Thus literally speaking it is not true that the creation of humanity is the high point – that belongs to the Sabbath day.[152] Indeed, why should the fact that we were the last created being in this account necessarily make us the most important? According to Hebrews 1, Jesus – the Son of God – is superior to angels; who, in turn, by virtue of the fact that the Hebrews passage was written to discourage the worship of Jesus as an angel, must be superior to humanity. Thus it is the Sabbath day that is important. For this is the day in which the human stands with the rest of creation and together they offer their praise to the creator whose creative breath brought them all into being. It is the day on which the whole of creation looks God-wards and recognizes that together they possess a theocentric heart.

The substantive model also finds it necessary to denigrate other non-human creatures[153] because of its insistence upon reason as being the most important God given human characteristic, and the supposedly logical extension that non-rational equals non-valuable. Douglas John Hall also illustrates how this same belief has also been responsible for the ill-treatment of children, the uneducated, the less civilized and even the female half of the race by those who choose to trust their own devilish definitions of reason.[154] The relational and functional views are also incomplete because they focus too

48

strongly upon the implications and miss the substance upon which their discoveries are based. Thus they both confuse the implications of the image with the image of God itself.

Although each of these views is incomplete in itself they can all provide us with essential insights into the meaning of this complex image. The image of God metaphor focuses first and foremost upon God and his total creation. The image is 'of God.' This frees us from a preoccupation with humankind and helps us see that the image is not so much connected to a capacity or potentiality within humanity for relationship, but is an expression of *God's* determination to have a relationship with us – and provides us with an example to follow in our attempts to emulate the creator. Mankind is *created* to stand before God; to be his counterpart on earth. He is also the appearance of God on earth; God's representative and co-creator. He is the conscious link between creator and the rest of creation: the God-intended mediator lifting the whole created universe up to God.[155] In this sense David Atkinson is correct to say that we are not so much 'human beings', as 'human becomings!'[156] Thus the image of God is not functional *per se* but enables mankind to fulfil the function of exercising dominion over the created order. It is not relational *per se* but enables mankind to relate to his creator, and thus fulfil the function of dominion in a manner which models 'the gracious and self-giving nature of the creator to each other and to the rest of creation.'[157]

These discoveries have a profound effect on our appreciation of the environment. Proponents of the substantive view were all too often steeped in a Greek world view which united a transcendent God with a low view of the non-human creation. The natural result was that our environment was reduced to the arena in which humans exerted their lordship. A hierarchical view of matter in which humanity is in total control naturally leads not only to the repression of the weak by the strong but also to the dehumanization of humanity since it asserts our independence from God (who is the very source of our humanity). This also de-sanctifies nature since it too is removed from its connectedness to its creator, from whom it derives its value.[158] Thus when humans are determined to be sub-human, the rest of creation feels the results because 'the solidarity of man with the rest of creation is so close that in some way or other nature must bear the consequences of men's sin'.[159]

The functional view has had a similar effect since the prevailing understandings of the God-given injunction to 'have dominion' have also been mainly Greek. The singularly most useful view has been the relational since it succeeds in stretching the mind beyond its usual human centred limits and introduces the possibility that the purpose of humanity might somehow lie beyond our own self-aggrandisement. When relationship is a possibility it becomes conceivable that God and humanity might somehow be able to fulfil *God's* destiny *together,* in two-way relationship. It might even be helpful to represent this relationship using the metaphor of the priest, since the priestly vocation is to stand between God and another (in this case his creation) in such a way as to interpret the good intentions of the creator to his creation and at the same time act on creation's behalf. But, helpful as it is, this view is not complete in itself. We also need to retain the substantive foundation and incorporate the future perspective of the functional view. It is only when we combine all three that we see the possibility that we might be capable of imaging God in a way which is in accord with the attractive character of God rather than our fallen nature. In short, this combined view gives us hope that mankind might learn to become responsible stewards under authority rather than tyrannical overlords.

I have now completed my look at what the bible teaches us about the nature of both the human and the non-human created order and its relationship with God. We have seen that non-human creation has inherent value, and have suggested that our ability to shape and mould our environment has been given us by God, since it is a consequence of us possessing his image. The very fact that we are creatures created in the image of God also has numerous implications for the way we live in God's creation, and confers many responsibilities upon us. The problem is that it is all too easy to see that this idealistic view does not represent reality. It seems that most of Western society is entrenched in ecologically unwise and economically greedy behaviour which, if the ideal is so perfect, makes it hard to understand why we make bad choices and stick to them come what may. In order to come to terms with reality we now need to move on and consider the effect of the Fall on the ideal.

Notes

1. William Hordern – in his article on Creation in *A Dictionary of Christian Theology*. ed. Alan Richardson. (SCM. London. 1969) p 79.

2. It has been common throughout Christian history for people to adopt the folk belief that since God is shrouded in mystery and cannot be fully understood, we come across him when we encounter things we don't understand or cannot explain. Prior to the Enlightenment, a God who was the sum of the gaps in our understanding had been immense and awesome. As human knowledge grew, and the gaps shrunk, the implication seemed to be that God was becoming smaller. Then as science pointed to the possibility of greater and greater control over the human environment the role for God became peripheral and many (including, famously, Laplace) came to consider him as unnecessary.

3. *Creatio ex Nihilo* is a latin term meaning that God created all things from nothing. Although creation *ex nihilo* is not an explicitly biblical doctrine, it was a concept which was adopted to counter the Platonic view that God is not so much creator as constructor, that he constructed the world out of pre-existent matter, and that he was therefore subject to and limited by material necessity, which was responsible for the universe's imperfections. The doctrine of creation *ex nihilo* was therefore, *inter alia*, an anti-duallistic insistence that matter should not be identified with evil.

4. Colin A. Russell – *Crosscurrents: Interactions Between Science and Faith*. (IVP Leicester. 1985) p 47.

5. William Paley published his popular book *Natural Theology* in 1802. In it he

argues that just as the intricacy and accuracy of a well-made watch implies that it has been designed for a particular purpose and presupposes the existence of an intelligent watchmaker, the adaption of each animal to its particular environment and needs presupposes a God who has created each one for its purpose.

6. In *Darwin's Forgotten Defenders: The Encounter between Evangelical Theology and Evolutionary Thought* (Eerdmans. Grand Rapids, Michigan and Scottish Academic Press. Edinburgh. 1987) David Livingstone writes: 'It was simply the nature of Darwin's metaphor that led him almost inevitably to fall back into vocabulary that was thoroughly anthropomorphic, purposive, teleological – and it was this element in his depiction of Nature that enabled evolution to be so readily elevated to mythological status.' (Livingstone, p 48)

7. Ibid. p 147. David Livingstone highlights the extent to which the clash between science and faith at the time of Darwin has been over-exaggerated. He lists many evangelical scientists and theologians who were prepared to deal openly and sympathetically with Darwin's theory and concludes that 'these problems were easily resolved by many evangelical scientists and theologians in the period as a variety of harmonizing models became available.' Livingstone. op. cit. p 51.

8. James Moore – *The Post-Darwinian Controversies: A study of the Protestant struggle to come to terms with Darwin in Great Britain and America 1870-1900.* (Cambridge University Press. Cambridge. 1979) p 303.

9. Russell. op. cit. (1985) p 150.

10. Ibid.

11. Quoted in Alec Vidler – *The Church in an Age of Revolution. 1789 to the present day.* (Penguin. London. 1971) p 121.

12. This is not the place for a full discussion of the creation/evolution debate. Readers are referred to R.J. Berry's book *God the Biologist and Evolution.* (Hodder & Stoughton.)

13. 'Natural theology' is the belief that all important elements of religion could be learned from created things, by reason alone.

14. Tony Lane – *The Lion Concise Book of Christian Thought.* (Lion. Tring. 1984) p 174.

15. Vidler. op. cit. (1971) p 125.

16. Not all Christians attacked Darwin. Some (mainly the evangelicals) recognized the danger of making another mistake akin to the (much earlier) attack on Copernicus. Colin Russell says. 'It was not that they failed to take scripture properly into account. Because they took it so seriously they declined to saddle it with arbitrary interpretations that flew in the face of empirical evidence.' Russell. op. cit. (1985) p 150.

17. E.g. Henri Blocher – *In the Beginning.* (IVP Leicester. 1984) pp 39-60.

18. See Ralph Venning – *The Plague of Plagues.* (First publ. 1669.) (Banner of Truth. London. 1965) This emphasis has been carried through to the present

day, where we see it in various forms and places. Westermann says. 'When the theology and the preaching of the Church are concerned only with salvation, when God's dealing with man is limited to the forgiveness of sins or to justification, the necessary consequence is that it is only in this context that man has to deal with God and God with man. This means that God is not concerned with a worm being trodden to the earth, or with the appearance of a new star in the Milky Way.' Claus Westermann – *Creation*. (SPCK London. 1974.) pp 3, 4.

19. The idea of God as 'first cause' was taken up by the Thomists (followers of Thomas Aquinas) who were keen on using metaphysical arguments to illustrate theological themes. Since scientific logic accepts that creation must have a first cause – even though up until now scientists have not been able to agree what this first cause was – such thinking was thought to create a role for God and therefore might have the potential to give a Christian faith some scientific justification.

20. Gerhard von Rad – *Genesis: A Commentary*. Revised edition. (SCM London. 1972) p 47-8.

21. Genesis 1:1.

22. See also Romans 1:20.

23. Millard Erickson. – *Christian Theology*. (Marshall Morgan and Scott. Basingstoke. 1987) p 348.

24. Donald MacKay – *The Clockwork Image*. (IVP. London. 1974) p 57.

25. James Houston – *I Believe in the Creator*. (Eerdmans. Grand Rapids, Michigan. 1980) p 57.

26. George Hendry – *Theology of Nature*. (Westminster Press. Philadelphia, Pennsylvania. 1980) p 119.

27. Plato. *Timaeus*. 29 E.

28. Alfred North Whitehead. – *Process and Reality*. (Macmillan. 1960) p 521. Process Theology is a theological system based on the works of Whitehead and Charles Hartshorne who couple a belief in evolutionary theory with an insistence that a God who is a continuing creator must be open to his creation to the extent that he learns from it and revises creation's potentialities as a result of what he learns.

29. Hendry. op. cit. (1980) p 122.

30. Acts 17:24, 25. 'The God who made the world and everything in it is the Lord of heaven and earth . . . and he is not served by human hands, as if he needed anything, because he himself gives all men life and breath and everything else.'

31. Francis Schaeffer – *Genesis in space and time*. (IVP. Wheaton, Illinois. 1972) p 26.

32. Von Rad. op. cit. (1972) p 52.

33. Deism was a system of thought which developed during the Enlightenment period. Its proponents insisted that reason was all that was needed to

demonstrate the rationality of belief in God; and since his power and intelligence were patently obvious to the human mind there was now no need for him to reveal himself in any other way. Indeed, if one adopts this view there is actually no need for God to remain involved with creation at all as long as he remains 'up there' and our minds can comprehend his being and interpret his intentions.

34. Hugh Montefiore (ed) – *Man and Nature.* (Collins. London. 1975) p 27.

35. See for example. Richard Dawkins – *The Blind Watchmaker.* (Penguin. 2000) and *Climbing Mount Improbable.* (Penguin. 1997). Also Jaques Monod – *Chance and Necessity.* (Knopf. New York. 1971)

36. See White. op. cit. (1967) p 1204.

37. Harvey Cox – *The Secular City. a celebration of its liberties and an invitation to its discipline.* (SCM. London. 1965)

38. Ibid. p 23.

39. Paulos Mar Gregorios in his essay 'New Testament foundations for understanding the Creation.' in Wesley Granberg Michaelson – *Tending the Garden. Essays on the Gospel and the Earth.* (Eerdmans. Grand Rapids, Michigan. 1987) p 86.

40. Paulos Mar Gregorios – *The Human Presence. An Orthodox View of Nature.* (WCC. Geneva. 1978) pp 19-22.

41. Houston. op. cit. (1980) p 50.

42. John 17:14.

43. e.g. 2 Corinthians 10:3; 1 John 2:15,17.

44. W.E. Vine – *Vine's Expository Dictionary of New Testament Words.* (McDonald. Virginia. undated) p 1256.

45. John A. T. Robinson – *Honest to God.* (SCM. London. 1963) p 56.

46. The Gaia Hypothesis was posited by James Lovelock in 1969 when he began working on the 'Goldilocks Problem' – discovering why the temperature of Venus is too hot for life, Mars too cold and the earth is right. Realizing that it was not a simple result of being the correct distance from the sun (the sun now burns up to 30 per cent hotter than it did when life first appeared on the planet), he suggested that some powerful self-regulating system was at the heart of the earth; with the planet itself acting as a large living organism producing 'feedback mechanisms' which correct imbalances and restore equilibrium.

47. Peter Russell – *The Awakening Earth.* (Routledge and Kegan Paul. London. 1982)

48. Ibid. p 130.

49. See Matthew Fox – *Original Blessing. A Primer in Creation Spirituality.* (Bear and Co. Santa Fe, New Mexico. 1983) and Lawrence Osborn – 'A Fox Hunter's Guide to Creation Spirituality.' in *Different Gospels. Christian Orthodoxy and Modern Theologies.* – Andrew Walker (ed) (Revised Edition SPCK. London. 1993.)

50. e.g. Genesis 1:26, John 1:1-3, Colossians 1:15-20.

51. Francis Schaeffer – *Pollution and the Death of Man. The Christian view of Ecology.* (Tyndale. Wheaton, Illinois. 1970) pp 30-33.
52. Panentheism is the belief that everything is *in* God.
53. Lawrence Osborn – 'A Fox Hunter's Guide to Creation Spirituality'. op. cit. p 160.
54. Ephesians 4:6.
55. John Polkinghorne – *Science and Christian Belief. Theological Reflections of a Bottom-Up Thinker.* (SPCK. London. 1994.) p 73.
56. Loren Wilkinson (ed.) – *Earthkeeping in the '90s.* (Eerdmans. Grand Rapids, Michigan. 1991) p 279.
57. See Genesis 3:14-20.
58. See the various laws in Leviticus etc.
59. Montefiore. op. cit. (1975) p 21.
60. Erickson. op. cit. (1987) p 368.
61. Francis Brown, S.R. Driver and Charles Briggs. *Hebrew and English Lexicon of the Old Testament.* (New York. Oxford University. 1955) p 135.
62. John Austin Baker – 'Biblical views of nature.' found in Birch, Eakin & McDaniel (eds.) – *Liberating Life. – Contemporary Approaches to Ecological Theology.* (Orbis Books. Maryland. 1990.) p 13.
63. Thomas Morris comments: 'This position is not usually thought by its proponents to be demonstrably true, but it is held to be a rational position to maintain . . . So whether it is derived from appeals to revelation or cosmological arguments, a belief in creation (*ex nihilo*) may well be rationally acceptable.' Thomas Morris – *Anselmian Explorations: Essays in Philosophical Theology.* (University of Notre Dame Press. Notre Dame, Indiana. 1987) pp 151, 160.
64. See von Rad. op. cit. (1972) p 51.
65. Werner Foerster in *Theological Dictionary of the New Testament.* ed. Kittel & Friedrich, transl. Geoffrey Bromiley. Vol 3. (Eerdmans. Grand Rapids. 1964-76). p 1029. Also see Matthew 13:35; 25:34; Mark 10:6; 13:19; Romans 1:20; Hebrews 1:10; Revelation 3:14 etc.
66. Foerster. op. cit. (1964-76) p 1025 and W.E. Vine. op. cit. p 256.
67. Hebrews 11:3.
68. Erickson. op. cit. (1987) p 370.
69. Albert Wolters – *Creation Regained.* (Eerdmans. Grand Rapids, Michigan. 1985) p 19.
70. See Ephesians 3:9; Colossians 1:16; Revelation 4:11.
71. Houston. op. cit. (1980) p 51.
72. Ibid. p 53.
73. *amar* is used in Gen 1:3,6,9 etc. and translated as 'said'.
74. Houston. op. cit. (1980) p 54.
75. John 1:1-3,14
76. John 1:5.

55

77. Revelation 4:11.

78. Erickson. op. cit. (1987) p 347.

79. Derek Kidner – *Genesis*. (IVP. Leicester. 1967) p 45.

80. Jürgen Moltmann – *God in Creation. An Ecological Doctrine of Creation*. (SCM. London. 1985) p 96.

81. Claus Westermann – *Genesis 1-11*. (SPCK. London. 1984.) p 87.

82. Schaeffer. op. cit. (1972) p 61ff.

83. The root verb to the word *shalom* is the verb 'to fill.' see Tim Marks – *His Light in Our Darkness*. (Kingsway. Eastbourne. 1988) p 16.

84. Wilkinson. op. cit. (1991) p 288.

85. Westermann. op. cit. (1984) p 87.

86. Jeanne Kay – 'Concepts of Nature in the Hebrew Bible.' *Environmental Ethics*. Winter 1988. Vol. 10. No 4. p 313. She compares Genesis 1:20 with Psalm 42:2-3.

87. Ecclesiastes 3:19, 21.

88. Kay. op. cit. (1988) p 313.

89. Genesis 2:7, 19.

90. George Caird – *Principalities and Powers: A Study in Pauline Theology*. (Clarendon Press. Oxford. 1956) p 65.

91. Ron Elsdon – *Greenhouse Theology*. (Monarch. Tunbridge Wells. 1992) p 34.

92. Ibid.

93. Westermann – *Creation*. (SPCK. London. 1974) p 62-64.

94. Job 38-41.

95. Psalm 104:24-25.

96. Westermann. op. cit. (1974) p 61.

97. Romans 8.

98. See, for example, Psalm 19.

99. Natural Revelation refers to the things we learn about God from creation and its laws and powers. Specific Revelation refers to things we could not learn about God if he had not given us law, scripture and Jesus. Louis Berkof – *Systematic Theology*. (Banner of Truth. Edinburgh. 1984) p 37.

100. See Acts 14:17; Romans 1:20.

101. A value is assigned to 'nature' by designating it as a 'free good' or 'public good' as opposed to 'private good' for which individuals are prepared to pay. A public good is something which society recognizes is of value, but needs to be paid for by everybody (usually via taxes) in order for its full benefit to be felt by all. Thus a value is assigned to 'public goods' like clean air, pure water, a credible defence force etc., and that value is equal to the amount which will be spent centrally in order to provide it. The limitation of both these terms is that they imply the 'free good' is almost an inalienable right, and since no payment is required there can be no enforceable restrictions on its use.

102. Sam Berry argues this point well in 'Environmental knowledge, attitudes and action. a code of practice.' *Scientific Public Affairs* 5(2), 1990. pp 16-17.

The Story of Creation

103. Fisher Humphreys – 'All creatures of our God and King.' (Beeson Divinity School. Birmingham, Alabama. 1991) p 3.
104. George Hendry. op. cit. (1980) pp 120-1.
105. Francis Schaeffer. op. cit. (1970) p 48.
106. Moltmann. op. cit. (1985) pp 77-78.
107. John Cobb Jr. – 'Postmodern Christianity in Quest for Eco-Justice.' in Deiter Hessel. (ed.) *After Nature's Revolt.* (Fortress Augsburg. Minneapolis, Minnesota. 1992) p 32-34.
108. Ibid. p 33.
109. Richard Russell – 'Creation and Conservation. The Ecological orientation of the Christian Faith. Part II' in *Biblical Creation.* 5:16. p 118.
110. White. op. cit. (1967) p 1205.
111. Günter Altner – 'The Community of Creation as a Community in Law. The New Contract between the Generations.' from *Concilium.* 1991/4. ed. Johann Baptist Metz & Edward Schillebeeckx. (SCM Press) p 55.
112. Moltmann. op. cit. (1985) p 31.
113. Houston. op. cit. (1980) p 74.
114. Von Rad. op. cit. (ed. Kittel & Friedrich 1964-76) p 390.
115. e.g. see Numbers 33:52.
116. Colossians 3:10. '(you) have put on the new self, which is being renewed in knowledge in the image of its creator.'
117. Irenaeus – *Adversus Haereses.* 5:6.1.
118. Thomas Aquinas – *Summa Theologica.* Part 1. Question 93.
119. Emil Brunner – *Man in Revolt.* (Westminster Press. Philadelphia. 1947) p 97.
120. Karl Barth – *Church Dogmatics.* Vol 3 Part 1. (T&T Clark. Edinburgh. 1958) p. 184.
121. Ibid. p 186.
122. John 17.
123. Luke 22:42; John 4:34; 5:30 etc.
124. Matthew 9:36; 10:6; John 8:1-11 etc.
125. Leonard Verduin – *Somewhat less than God: The Biblical view of Man.* (Eerdmans. Grand Rapids, Michigan. 1970) p 27.
126. See Genesis 9:6; James 3:9-10.
127. The name Tutankhamun means 'The living image of Amon.' See Henri Blocher – *In the Beginning.* (IVP. Leicester. 1984) p 86/7.
128. e.g. Col. 3:10-12. We will be looking at the effect of the fall on the Image of God in the next part.
129. See Genesis 3:1-5.
130. See Catherina Halkes – *New Creation. Christian Feminism and the Renewal of the Earth.* (SPCK. London. 1991) p 130.
131. Blocher. op. cit. (1984) p 85.
132. See 1 Corinthians 11:7; 2 Corinthians 3:18.

133. See Exodus 20:4-6.
134. Matthew 22:21.
135. See Colossians 3:1-11.
136. See Mark 12:28-31.
137. e.g. See James 3:9; 1 John 4:20.
138. Luke 3:38.
139. Acts 17:28.
140. Moltmann. op. cit. (1985) p 220.
141. Westermann. op cit. (1974) p 56.
142. Ibid. p 217.
143. Rowland Moss – *The Earth in Our Hands.* (IVP. Leicester. 1982) p 34ff.
144. Genesis 2:7. 'And the Lord God formed man from the dust of the ground.' The Hebrew for 'man' (Adam) sounds like the Hebrew for 'ground' (adamah) and may be related. Loren Wilkinson comments. 'What the words and the whole account suggest, then, is what contemporary biologists and ecologists have been trying hard to tell us. whatever else we are, humans are also *earth*; we share our nature with its soil, its plants, its animals.' Wilkinson. op. cit. p 284.
145. Douglas John Hall – *Imaging God. Dominion as Stewardship.* (Friendship Press & Eerdmans. New York & Grand Rapids, Michigan. 1986) p 69.
146. Genesis 2:7,19.
147. Genesis 1:29,30.
148. Genesis 1:27,28a. Interestingly this tension also divided Plato and Aristotle. Although they were in agreement that it was rationality that separated man from the animal kingdom, Plato insisted that man's uniqueness meant that he was outside of nature, whereas Aristotle believed we were a special part of it.
149. Moltmann. op. cit. (1985) p 218.
150. Westermann. op. cit. (1974) p 56.
151. Hall. op. cit. (1986) p 67.
152. Most commentators agree that the sabbath day is the high point of the creation story. See for example. David Atkinson – *The Message of Genesis 1-11.* (IVP. Leicester. 1990) p 43. von Rad. op. cit. p 61ff. Von Rad says. 'But what sense can there be in mentioning one further matter *above* and *beyond* the creation of the entire cosmos and all living creatures? And this matter is obviously of such significance that it is ranked above all the rest, and forms the final conclusion to the whole . . . Furthermore it is significant that God 'completed' his work on the seventh day and not, as it seems more logical, on the sixth.' p 62.
153. See for example. Humphreys. op. cit. p 2. & Robert Whelan – *Mounting Greenery – A Short view of the Green Phenomenon.* Chapter 7. (Institute of Economic Affairs. Education Unit. London. Sept. 1989)
154. Hall. op. cit. (1985) p 108-110.

155. See Paulos Mar Gregorios – The Human Presence. op. cit. (1978) p 64,5.

156. Atkinson – *The Message of Genesis* (IVP. Leicester. 1990) p 39.

157. Wilkinson. op. cit. (1991) p 286.

158. Philip Sherrard – *The Rape of Man and Nature*. (Golgonooza Press. 1987) p 90.

159. Caird. op. cit. (1914) p 65-6.

CHAPTER TWO

~

The Story of the Fall

The Importance of the Fall

In the first chapter I concentrated upon the world as it was created to be. I have done this in the belief that 'an environmental perspective must be built on what should be rather than on what is. The intention of creation is our rightful focus.'[1] It is only as we understand what harmony meant to the creation that it becomes possible to appreciate the full implications of the Fall upon the created order. Without this 'prelapsarian' perspective we also remain unaware of what to hope for, and our hope of redemption becomes nothing to look forward to.

H. Paul Santmire is convinced that Christian theology is not the inherently destructive influence Lynn White claims it to be. In a paper written eight years after White's article,[2] and later in his book entitled *The Travail of Nature*[3] Santmire points out that although the Reformation traditions of both Luther and Calvin were focused firmly on God and man,[4] they did not exclude nature. Indeed, practically speaking:

> The God confessed by the Reformers was . . . powerfully, majestically, and immediately involved in all the processes of nature, as well as in the affairs of human and ecclesiastical history . . . Thus the Reformers' view of the human creature . . . has an underlying ecological character, like their view of God.[5]

Thus Santmire concludes that in its earliest stages, Reformation theology had a

> pronounced and pervasive ecological dimension . . . The Reformation tradition did approach a state of ecological bankruptcy more and more, however, as it became locked in with

the forces of modern science, modern philosophy, and modern industrialism . . . But is it historically legitimate, for that reason, to blame the parent tradition, without extensive qualification, for the behaviour of the child? In particular, is the Reformation tradition as a whole ecologically bankrupt, because its latter day children have been such ecological delinquents? The answer to this question, without any special pleading, must clearly be 'No.'[6]

Thus, whilst Santmire concedes that there was a relationship between Capitalism and Calvinism, he believes that it is folly to suppose that the Western theological tradition is even the major influence upon our ecologically destructive behaviour. I believe that Welbourn is right when he says that the mood of the last century was such that men like Bacon and Boyle who were at the forefront of scientific and technological progress still had to show how their discoveries *could be justified* by the bible in order to gain Christian respectability; despite the fact that their drive was essentially a humanist one.[7] He adds that it is only since the 1940s that Western humanity no longer felt it necessary to find biblical justification for our actions. This is not to suggest that the drive was wrong *per se*, but it indicates how, all too often, the moral basis for innovation is sought to fit the discovery after it has been made.

Furthermore, examination of the facts makes it impossible to agree with White that the worst environmental damage is limited to Christian cultures.[8] Peacocke and Passmore cite Japan as the perfect example of an excessively destructive culture which has never been committed to a distinctively monotheistic religion.[9] This suggests that one of White's central theses that Christian theology spawned the growth of science and technology which went on to provide the means of dominating the earth, is not entirely correct.[10] In fact, Christians through the ages have very often been in the anti-technological lobby, and have been ridiculed for being such insistent critics.[11] Santmire believes that the most important question that needs to be asked is why figures such as Kant, Galileo, Descartes and Newton seized upon their preferred interpretation of Genesis 1:26-8 and ignored the texts that teach justice and respect. In other words, why 'has the modern West as a matter of course read the Bible through the eyes of Adam Smith rather than St Francis?'[12]

Perhaps Lynn White's greatest mistake was that he failed to take account of the tendency of men and women to live as though there were no restraint on their freedom. Thus the simple fact that men like Bacon, Newton and Galileo had an interest in theology, and believed that their scientific exploits would lead them closer to God's mind, is enough for White to make the conclusion that these men were pursuing a science that was 'cast in the matrix of Christian theology.'[13] But a deduction that the reasons and motives of anyone who claimed a Christian faith could be entirely pure and fully devoted to the practice of their religion is too simplistic. What is more, there is never one simple Christian understanding on any issue – every theologian and individual Christian sees things slightly differently, depending on his presuppositions and a variety of cultural factors. And even if there were one clear 'Christian' view on the value of the environment, the bible tells us that even the most devoted follower of Christ identifies with the experience of the apostle Paul, who writes about his constant struggle to do right; and about the temptation to assert the human will over and above the will of God.[14] The reason for this, according to the bible, is that mankind has fallen from fellowship with God, and now lives in a twilight zone in which a relationship with the creator is possible, but is fraught with frustration and misunderstanding.

Although the doctrine of the Fall is right at the heart of biblical teaching, not all attempts to discover an environmentally caring theology give it the importance it is due. Both the Anglican symposium headed by Hugh Montefiore[15] and the ideas of pantheist thinkers like Matthew Fox minimize the Fall – albeit for different reasons. Fox abandons the doctrine because he associates it with 'gloomy Puritanism' which he insists played such an important part in devaluing and then exploiting nature.[16] He believes that it is by re-sanctifying nature and divinizing the cosmos (or rather recognizing that it is already divine), and by abandoning the ideas of fall and sin that creation will free itself from its shackles. But this does not really help us discover why things are as we find them; and simply turning to nature does not help us find the key to either its value or its meaning. 'Without the Fall, we would be left, not with the benignity of "original blessing", but instead the terror of evil and suffering regarded as necessary outcomes of evolutionary experimentation.'[17] In a pantheist world it becomes impossible both to distinguish good from evil and to explain their presence adequately, and it also becomes harder to make choices between wise and foolish behaviour.[18]

In Montefiore's *Man and Nature*, the two theological parts within the report section of the book focus on 'creation' and 'salvation'. They are linked by a three page statement acknowledging only 'residual truth' in the doctrine of a cosmic Fall; and stating the writer's belief that to accept the full doctrine somehow places a question mark against the idea that the earth was created by a loving God. According to the report 'Christian theology does not teach simply a doctrine of creation, but links creation indissolubly to redemption and sanctification.'[19] This statement is true but fails to recognize that creation and salvation have to be linked by the Fall in order for salvation to mean anything other than God completing what he did not do right first time. Not only is it essential to understand the meaning of creation's brokenness before we are able to understand its destiny, but it is only when we take the Fall seriously that it becomes possible to attach any meaning to salvation which is, after all, about the overcoming of these forces. For this reason I am convinced that studying the full impact of the Fall on humanity and nature will help us to understand the potential depth of the Christian contribution to our subject. We will then have built a platform from which mankind can work with God in the task of radical recreation.

The Problem of Evil
The Christian is forced to live with a fundamental tension right at the heart of his theology. Of course some have tried to deal with the problem by adopting a view similar to the Christian Scientist position that ills such as sickness and death are illusory but this is not credible in the face of the overwhelming evidence![20] The difficulty arises when we try and reconcile the bible's teaching that God is both all-powerful and perfectly loving with the existence of evil in the created order.

The dualist answer to this dilemma is to insist that there are two forces in the universe. God, as the good force, and another (uncreated) evil influence. The God in this system is engaged in a battle against evil, but is limited in his power to control it. Thus the final outcome is always unsure, and God is forced to work with and adapt to events as he finds them. But explaining the presence of evil by compromising God's omnipotence might explain why evil exists, but it provides no hope that it will be overcome.

A second approach to the problem is to modify our understanding of God's goodness. A way to do this is by adopting a determinist attitude which insists that nothing happens that is not willed by God. This means that God can be seen as the ultimate cause of what we call evil, whilst at the same time, men and women are responsible and accountable for the acts they commit. Millard Erickson explains the logic of this position when he represents it as follows:

Whatever happens is caused by God.
Whatever is caused by God is good.
Whatever happens is good.[21]

In this attempted solution, our understanding of God has been so defined that it is impossible to call God 'good' in the way we usually understand the meaning of that term. God's will seems to us to be both arbitrary and impossible to thwart. As to why God is good, the only reason we are left with is the fact that *he* has defined himself as such, and there is no higher arbiter to judge otherwise. Likewise, evil can similarly be defined away – where it is our limited perspective which wrongly labels things or experiences as evil, simply because we cannot see them from God's viewpoint.

The Pantheist standpoint on evil is to insist that since everything is divine, evil only exists where there is a dislocation of part of God from its divine centre. There can only be an end to evil when all matter is absorbed back into God and finds its harmony restored. A theist who sees all things as evolving towards perfection, on the other hand, will see chaos, pain and destruction in the created order as an inevitable part of the evolutionary process – like growing pains – but few will believe it appropriate to describe these experiences as evil.

Process theologians deal with the problem by insisting that God has put freedom at the heart of his creation, and chooses to offer a starting vision along with a drive to achieve it. But the key to God's creation is the freedom each creature is given 'to actualize the best possibility open to it'.[22] Ruth Page comments that this removes the problem of evil from a theological issue to a practical one, given that freedom will inevitably produce conflicts and mistakes along the way.[23]

The difficulty is that only the last of these views gives any indication as to how or why evil exists, and even that gives little hope that there is any purpose in suffering or a God who is in direct control. For each of them evil is simply part of the world around us and there is little we can do about it except, in the latter cases, live with it and absorb it into our beings as we evolve towards our divine destiny. Such attempts to think of evil as a necessary or even beneficial part of God's creation run into difficulties in so far as they do not account for the sheer quantity of evil and suffering in the world; just as they fail to cope either with suffering which seems so entirely meaningless or with the suffering of the innocent. It is hard to conceive of such a process as being worth the cost; and if the 'innocent' include the animal kingdom it seems rather arrogant to see the suffering of animals as a means to the end of human maturity and growth. These views also fail to give us any indication as to how we can work with God as people created in his image, and as those who have been entrusted with the task of stewarding the earth.

The Story of the Fall
In Genesis 3, and the account of the Fall, we find a story of an event which leaves the picture of harmony far behind. Adam and Eve exercise their gift of freewill and opt out of a relationship of dependence upon their creator in favour of independence. The crash happens as all relationships within creation are thrown into confusion.

Although, generally speaking, I am happy to follow the traditional designation of Genesis 3 as 'The Fall,' it should now be made clear that what I am referring to by using this term is not a (dualist) sudden metaphysical change within humans or creation from a spiritual to a material plane, but rather the fact that mankind chose, and continues to choose, to overstep a limit prescribed for us by God. Perhaps, if we are inclined to agree with William Dumbrell that the creation account represented a covenant between us and God, we could see the events described as Adam's breaking of this original covenant.[24]

Certainly Hosea seems to support this idea.[25] If this is the case, the Fall is from covenant relationship and blessing, and towards alienation from God and loss of identity.

'You must not eat . . . for when you eat of it you will surely die'

There can be no sin unless there is first a prohibition. Von Rad believes this interdiction to be completely motivated by God's care and concern for humanity whom he has created in his image and given the task to care for his creation.[26] So verse 17 is the wise and concerned advice of a Father who then ensures that Adam has the partner he needs both to help him, and in order that the human race might be as productive as the garden they tend. The verse contains both a command and a warning. The fact that God issues the command makes it clear to Adam that he is, in fact, able to do anything he wishes. It is supposed that this free will is derived both from the likeness of God within us, and the creator's desire to have a relationship with Adam and his descendants based on choice. The warning indicates that God expects Adam's free will to keep him inside the covenant, and so he places limits upon Adam's freedom, the voluntary acceptance of which is intended to ensure both that Adam accepts the delineation between creator and creation, and that he also recognizes there is a price to be paid for disobedience.

'The serpent said to the woman . . . '

Although it has been common practice for interpreters to make a link between the serpent and Satan, both von Rad and Westermann insist that it is wrong to make too close an identification. For sure, the enemy of God is to be seen behind the events of the Fall, but to place too great an importance on the figure of the serpent is to risk absolving humanity from the blame for its disobedience. The snake is a created creature

which had been named by Adam,[27] and is used as the bringer
of temptation so as to 'guard against objectifying evil in any
way, therefore [the writer] has personified it as little as possible
as a power coming from without.'[28]

Thus von Rad and Westermann are insisting that the use of a
simple, but crafty, serpent serves to warn us against pitying Eve
by making too much of the power of her adversary. Eve was not
forced into sin, but was tempted and gave in willingly. Thus the
use of the snake reveals weakness in mankind, and shows that
'at the very moment the sinner is intoxicated with the sense of
his own power, he is being manipulated by *another* mind. In
actual fact, sin is defeat.'[29]

Henri Blocher suggests that the fact the snake was part of the
very animal kingdom over which Adam and Eve were to have
dominion indicates that

> orders established at creation are being twisted and smashed with
> the violation of the divine covenant, either directly in the
> commission of the offence, or else in its repercussions (as the
> continuation of the narrative will show). Sin is accompanied by
> an alteration of the original hierarchies and harmonies.[30]

Perhaps this is an early indication of the difficulties that are
to come in our attempts to exercise stewardship justly – it is
not only *our* sin which leads to tyrannical behaviour, but the
problems are compounded by a fallen creation that fails to
function as it should.

The use of an anonymous snake, and the fact that the snake
is not interrogated by God in verse 13 is also thought by
Westermann to indicate that the writer of the account is
making no attempt to explain the origin of evil in this story.[31]
He suggests it is even possible that the conversation with the
snake is a means of giving physical form to a process of mental
reasoning going on in Eve's mind. Whatever the case, the
central message of this passage is that 'evil is not the good that

God has created, but the rejection of the order that God has instituted for the enjoyment of the world.'[32] Evil is a fact, and wherever the seeds originated, the account suggests that it entered creation at the point at which Adam and Eve choose to assert their wills and go their own way. This opens the way for a redemption that begins with a recognition of human willfulness and a willingness to realign ourselves with God's estimation of what is right, which necessarily leads to right action.

'Did God really say you must not eat? . . . '

The identity of the snake is by no means as important as its words. The question posed by the serpent is a deliberate distortion of the creator's words which succeeds in making Eve over-confident in her reply, thus lulling her into a false sense of security. In her over-assuredness Eve overstates the command, and adds 'and you must not touch it' to God's words. At this point it is as if the tempter senses the weakness of Eve's position and he moves in for the kill. He now shows that he is not interested in knowing what God had commanded, but in leading Eve to doubt God and his good intentions. Even the snake's denial that 'Dying you shall not die'[33] leaves open the possibility that what looks like death might actually lead to life.[34] Eve accepts the invitation to assess God's command, and consider the implied possibility that God is being selfish and repressive. As she does so, the serpent feeds in the picture of a God who has not told her the whole truth, alongside the possibility that by eating the fruit she might become like God herself.

And this is important, because it is not an evil tree from which Eve ate, but the 'tree of the knowledge of good and evil'. The most important thing to note about the idea of 'knowledge' in these verses, is that the serpent is referring to the kind of 'knowledge of that which is useful or harmful to man.'[35] Such knowledge is not just an intellectual *'gnosis'* or the ability to make moral decisions, but is 'know how', knowledge about how to be independent and what has good and bad effects. And fallen humanity is always tempted to regard such knowledge as wisdom – something the Old Testament wisdom literature declares impossible to attain apart from God.[36] So in this context 'knowledge of good and evil means... omniscience in the widest sense of the word.'[37]

It is possible that this is an early example of the literary device called *'merismus'* whereby paired opposites (in this example, good and evil) are used together to denote totality. If this is the case, the tree represents *all* knowledge. This, together with the fact that in Canaanite culture the snake was a commonly used symbol of occult knowledge, makes it certain that the recorded longing for this kind of knowledge is meant to indicate an underlying desire to be independent from God, and make (presumably better) decisions based on this new ability to know.

> What the serpent's insinuation means is the possibility of an extension of human existence beyond the limits set for it by God at creation, an increase in life not only in the sense of pure intellectual enrichment but also, of familiarity with, and power over, mysteries that lie beyond man.[38]

'The woman saw... so she took some and ate it'

As she takes time to reflect on the fruit and its allure, Eve's evaluation is that it seems as if all the serpent has told her is true. She agrees that the forbidden fruit does look attractive, and begins to desire that which indeed seems to be beneficial to her. Blocher thinks these details are important because they emphasize the fact that it is always that which is genuinely beautiful that attracts us into seizing and misusing it – thus perverting and destroying what was once good in God's sight. This seems to give another helpful perspective on the debate into the origin of evil, where it becomes clear that nothing is intrinsically bad – but becomes fallen when it is misappropriated by those who are driven by their own chosen and sinful desires. It is the *knowledge* of both good and evil and the resulting schizophrenia that distorts us and drives us mad. Thus at the heart of temptation is the invitation 'to invert the order established by the Father.'[39]

The act of taking and eating is almost underplayed, as if the writer wishes us to conclude that the event is 'almost as something self-evident, inwardly consistent,'[40] or 'completely natural, and (now) perfectly human.'[41] Eve does not need to persuade or trick Adam into sharing the fruit: he willingly follows her example. It is Adam's active complicity in this sin that forbids us to make too much of the fact that Eve was the one who made the first choice, as if this proves that women are more liable to sin than men. Perhaps there is something to be said for the fact that God gave the command to Adam, and by virtue of Eve receiving it as a second generation command it had not got the same hold over her. But this does not absolve Adam, because in verse 6 we read that he 'was with her'. Thus in allowing Eve to debate with the snake Adam was evading the responsibility that God had placed upon him to ensure that his instructions were obeyed. However we apportion the blame, both Adam and Eve are held equally accountable in the judgement which comes later, and Adam cannot shift his guilt by blaming Eve.[42] Claus Westermann is convinced that the most important lesson to learn from this is that 'human community in its basic form . . . can lead to fulfilment together and to sin together.'[43]

The result is that in their shame Adam and Eve seek to conceal that which their unauthorized knowledge has revealed to them. But their coverings do no good, and as God enters the scene (the fact that he does not 'come down' but is walking in the garden emphasizes the previous closeness between creator and mankind) Adam hides because he is now afraid of his nakedness. They are ashamed because their new knowledge has unmasked the truth about themselves. Previously they were guiltless and felt no shame at their nakedness,[44] but now they are driven to hide themselves from each other and from God because they have been found out.

'Adam, where are you?...'

That which had once been Adam's crowning glory – his unique capacity for fellowship with God – now becomes something of which to be afraid. Adam cannot remain hidden from God, and has to admit his fear, and ultimately his disobedience. The claim to know good and evil has divided Adam at the very centre of his being. The knowledge he has discovered was not previously unknown to God; rather it was hidden from Adam because God wished to protect him from the consequences of it. The story illustrates how we have reached into a world which we had believed would then be our own creation, only to find that it does not possess the same inherent goodness as that which was previously offered us by the creator. In rejecting the givenness of our being in favour of autonomy, Adam discovers only inner shame, which causes him to hide from the fact that he has lost the knowledge of his true self which can only be discovered within a relationship with his creator. This is what Tim Marks means when he says:

> Man in his fallen state is not a whole being. The fractures made by sin run not only through our relationship with God and with our fellow men, but also within ourselves. We do not understand who we are – we are a mystery... The fractures of the mind are caused partly because we see the world from our perspective rather than God's. They are also the result of the way in which people's sinful and self-orientated choices have impinged on our lives. We are wounded, broken people crying for help from the hurt within. We are people who are on the run, fleeing from

emotions of rage and lust and greed. We dare not face who we are, we cannot name the thing we have become.[45]

Adam and Eve are presented as the forerunners of a race who, in the search for more knowledge, have lost what knowledge they had about who they are and what they were created to become. This fear before God and the shame before each other (as well as the double attempts to shift the blame) reveal that the two most fundamental relationships within creation are now disordered even before God pronounces his judgement. The force of this revelation points to the fact that the seeds of disorder have already sprouted. This suggests that God's decree in verses 14-19 is as much about him revealing to Adam and Eve the natural implications of their actions as a considered response to their disobedience. Adam and Eve were made to be dependent upon their creator's ongoing blessing and benevolence, but they chose to cut the ties and assert their independence. From that moment on, all human activities lose their identification with a central point of reference and the whole idea of there being a system of justice and harmony based around absolute standards within creation becomes blurred. Thus all relationships are thrown into confusion, including that between humans and the rest of creation.

'Because you have done this . . . '
The purpose of the interrogation and trial is to reveal to Adam and Eve the implications of what they have done. This, as I have just suggested, seems to be aimed at helping us understand why we, and the world in which we live, are in such turmoil. Using a series of questions and answers, the writer uncovers the facts and makes it quite clear that we are still responsible to God and answerable for our actions even though we might wish it otherwise. Likewise, God still cares for people from whom he is now estranged. In God's second question recorded in verse 11 he reveals that first and foremost

this act of defiance was a sin against God, and is therefore an act which carries consequences which are both just and logical.[46]

As the three judgements are pronounced, we note that they each reflect the character and nature of the offender. The snake is cursed. This is a fate which is not repeated in the other two judgements and is probably in line with the understanding elsewhere in the Old Testament that the punishment we read here promises the eventual overthrow of the forces of evil which the snake represents.[47] After all, it is the snake who is the adversary, and it is its plan to war against God which has been discovered and punished.

> One must, under all circumstances, proceed from the fact that the passage reflects quite realistically man's struggle with the real snake; but one must not stop there ... thus by a serpent he understands not only the zoological species, but at the same time, ... in a kind of spiritual clearheadedness, he sees in it a kind of evil being that has assumed form, that is inexplicably present within our created world, and that has singled out man, lies in wait for him, and everywhere fights a battle with him for life and death. The serpent is an animal which, more than any other, embodies uncanny qualities that make it superior to man.[48]

In addition to humiliating the snake for his rebellious act, God also announces that there will now be a permanent hostility between human and serpent which will ensure that they will never again collaborate in such a destructive way. Henri Blocher believes that this enmity is maintained by a deep-seated horror at the evil the snake tricked Eve into opening the door to.

Finally God spells out the eventual fate of the forces of evil. The seed of the woman will crush the snake's head – an image which spells out final defeat. Claus Westermann is uneasy at reading a Messianic promise into this text for the reason that, in his opinion, the word 'seed' can only refer to the succession of descendants and not an individual. But given the fact that Matthew 1 makes much of Jesus' line of ancestry including figures such as Abraham, Isaac, Jacob, David and the like; I do not consider that it is too far-fetched to suggest that the whole genealogy could be said to have played its part in Jesus' final humiliation of the power of evil in the world.

But whilst Westermann might well be correct in asserting that the original meaning of the passage was not a prophecy or promise of the coming Messiah,[49] the New Testament at least sees this verse as being a shadow of God's future salvation.[50] It therefore seems right to retain at least the possibility that this verse might be a foreshadowing of the Christ because the verse which states that the snake shall have its head crushed also has a 'symbolic implication, for *ros* (head) also means 'principle', 'essence', 'sum' and 'summit'. The adversary will be totally vanquished.'[51]

The second judgement falls on Eve and affects her role as mother and wife. It is significant that God does not wipe out the human race but renews his blessing and command for them to be fruitful. But this blessing of fruitfulness now has added difficulties for Eve and her descendants, and the blessing becomes a burden at the very point at in which she is most unique – her ability to bear children. Eve's role as wife is affected in a similar way. She was given to Adam to be a helper in his task of tilling the earth, and so that they might both enjoy the benefits of partnership. It seems natural to presume that the reason none of the animals was suitable was because the creator intended this relationship to be one between complementary equals. After the Fall the two continue to be attracted to each other, but it is their ability to complement each other that is affected. Previously Eve's created purpose was to function in partnership with her husband and to be treated justly, their physiological differences not meaning that they have different rights. The perversion of this order is seen in the use of the word 'desire', and in the phrase 'and he will rule over you.'

Most commentators see the word 'desire' as referring to a desire *of* the woman *for* her husband. It is not necessary to see this as being primarily a sexual drive – rather a longing to find fulfilment and rest with her intended soul mate.[52] But this is not the only possibility since the word translated 'desire' in verse 16, and which is only used in two other places in scripture,[53] means 'a desire to dominate' when it is used in Genesis 4. Since this translation would parallel 'rule over' later in verse 16, there is probably good reason to take this domineering spirit as being the intention here. Thus the new tendency will be for both man and wife to vie for control of their relationship, but with the husband being able to abuse his physical strength and exploit his wife's sense of commitment to him – turning a harmonious relationship of equality into one of strife. This does not have the character of precept in post-Fall societies, but is simply a recognition of the kind of behaviour unchecked human nature will gravitate towards. Thus the very relationship which was meant to bring complementary parties together around a common goal is now fractured by sin – to the detriment of the goal itself.

These punishments do not mean that the woman ceases to find fulfilment in her honoured status as wife and mother.[54] Rather it is

> just where the woman finds her fulfilment in life, her honour and her joy, namely in her relationship to her husband and as mother of her children, there too she finds that it is not pure bliss, but pain, burden, humiliation and subordination.[55]

The final judgement is directed at Adam and his role in seeking a livelihood in order to provide for his family.[56] However, this time it does not just affect Adam alone. The punishment changes the earth upon which Adam works.

A mutual recalcitrance now breaks into creation as a profound disorder. Man was taken from the earth and so was directed to it; she was the material basis of his existence; a solidarity of creation existed between man and the ground. But a break occurred in this affectionate relationship, an alienation that expresses itself in a silent, dogged struggle between man and soil. Now it is as though a spell lay on the earth which makes her deny man the easy produce of subsistence.[57]

Again there is the hint of wordplay here since Adam's condemnation relates to his relationship with the earth (*adama*). Adam is still intended to cultivate the earth, but again, the work which was part of God's unique blessing upon him now becomes toil.[58] This means that work is frustrating – the intended fruit of human activity is now choked by the unwelcome weeds and undergrowth.[59] Every harvest demands sweat; and whilst work still retains an element of blessing since agricultural success is still possible, this passage presents humanity and nature as relating together in a newly dis-harmonized manner.

The Fall and Human Destiny

God's threat in Genesis 2 was that if Adam was disobedient to this single command he would 'surely die'. The actual punishment is found in 3:19, which in turn has provided the grounds for much debate on the origin and purpose of death. It is true that this is the first reference to the existence of physical death in Genesis; but we cannot suppose that there is any indication that the writer was making any particular point about the origin of death. He simply mentions it in passing. The main subject of the verse is the difficulty of human attempts to farm the soil; and the plain meaning of the text is that toil only ends when life itself is finished. In other words the verse simply states that work is part and parcel of total human existence. However, even if the writer did not intend these words to be interpreted as a theological statement about the origin of death, verse 19 provides us with a useful springboard from which we can debate whether the whole passage suggests that death is a separate punishment brought about by the Fall.

In the New Testament Paul states that, for humans, death is a direct consequence of sin.[60] Consequently, many commentators suggest this implies that prior to the Fall humans were inherently immortal. This view is probably influenced by two factors, the influence of the Greek doctrine of the immortality of the soul, and a strong desire to make the difference between pre- and post-Fall humanity as great as possible. But this view gives rise to a difficulty. How would overcrowding have been prevented if Adam and Eve had not fallen and humans had continued to obey the command to be fruitful and fill the earth? Perhaps God's plan would have been to translate people into his presence without them experiencing death – in much the same way as he rewarded Enoch and Elijah.[61]

Claus Westermann is reluctant to make the passage say something it was not written to express. He says that since the main point of the passage is to indicate that human work is burdensome from birth to death, it is gratuitous to read a statement about the origin of death into it.[62] Von Rad agrees, and adds that if this mention of death is to be seen as a punishment, it is so only in the sense that it is the first time Adam's final fate is revealed to him. But:

> whatever the case of man's mortality or immortality may otherwise have been, this statement would never have been addressed to man in such a way *before* his sinning, and therefore it thematically belongs with special emphasis to the penalty.[63]

This is punishment simply because we now live with a constant reminder of our destiny hung round our neck like a millstone – which presumably saddled Adam with feelings of apathy and meaninglessness which made progress even harder to achieve. But von Rad concedes that there is a difficulty with this position in as far as the punishment, as he reads it, does not square with God's threat of death in Genesis 2:17. This he puts down to God's grace.

Blocher prefers to take the threat more seriously, and finds a solution in the work of Van Hoonacker which uses 1 Kings 2:36-46 as a parallel passage. He finds that 1 Kings renders the same Hebrew words as 'on that day you will fall under the power of a death sentence.'[64] Thus this verse is not promising immediate physical death (so explaining why Adam and Eve did not die there and then) but points to a new state in which from that point on everything is seen from a different perspective. Blocher is convinced that Paul also seems to read the passage in this way[65] when he describes death as God's punishment for sin. So we are not just talking about physical death as a punishment here; for, as von Rad concedes, Adam and Eve remained alive after the sentence. In fact, it is a fair assumption that death existed in some form or other in the garden prior to the Fall for God's prohibition to have made any sense to Adam.[66] Natural death would not have come about as a result of the moral fall but the Fall into being of space and time.

But the play on words between Adam and '*adama*' does seem to indicate that we are meant to see the Fall as the moment at which the reality of death entered into human experience, since it was from dust that Adam was created, and to that dust he now returns. Something has changed. Just as life is so much more than physical existence, so death here means much more than a physical end to life. It is also a symbol of spiritual and moral death. Adam's return to dust is an indication that it is the dual nature of humanity which is affected by this death – meaning that the image within us is somehow marred in such a way as to make our links with the dust stronger than our likeness to God. We are now destined to live lives that are characterized by death, and which actually bring the stench of death to our surroundings. As the image bearer of God it was not Adam's destiny to experience spiritual death. But his rebellion forfeited the intimate relationship with the creator that was previously his by right. In this case death really is 'the great exposure.'[67]

The Fall and Human Nature

One of the most important messages of the creation story was the idea that humanity is uniquely created in the image of God. The reason we were given this image was so that we could fulfil our calling to be in relationship with the creator, and in order that that this relationship could enable us to perform our unique function – to tend and care for the earth as God's ambassadors.

The first affirmation we need to make is that the image of God in mankind was not lost at the Fall since reference to the image of God appears in two contrasting contexts in both the Old and New Testaments. On the one hand there are passages which refer to the continuance of the image of God within humanity,[68] but there are also New Testament passages that clearly speak of the renewal of God's image in believers.[69] It becomes possible to weave these two strands together by focusing on the idea that although the post-Fall image is distorted, it was not lost when Adam and Eve fell into sin. In other words mankind still has a God-given personality which, to a limited extent, reflects the creator; and he has a potentiality for relationship with the God in which the image can be continually refined.

Returning to Genesis 3, we are reminded that the temptation to become like God led to actions which brought about the opposite result. Yet we still possess pretensions to deity, and in exalting ourselves we often produce the most extreme forms of cruelty which both deny the rights of other humans created in the same image, and abuse the non-human creation. It is especially ironic that in order to escape the moral boundaries put in place by God, we have to marginalize the very idea of a creator, and deify ourselves instead. But the act of removing true deity produces a one-dimensional spiritual world which actually makes us merely human. And 'the assertion that we are *merely* human result[s] in a dehumanization possibly without parallel in the history of the world.'[70] Larry Rasmussen highlights the irony of this when he indicates how both capitalist and Marxist philosophy hailed the control of nature by science, and looked ahead to the time when we would be more fulfilled and secure once this had been achieved. But the only promise the pursual of this hope has delivered is that 'we, as part of nature, may end up the most pathetic victims of this particular quest for power.'[71]

This loss of self-identity and the resultant need for a new identity from somewhere outside of themselves led Adam's descendants to build a tower as a monument to their own glory.[72] Although the intention was to build 'to the heavens,' the story tells of God still having to come down to examine their work; and we then read of God's judgement on this tower built with human materials and with human ingenuity. In his judgement 'God makes it abundantly clear that he will not tolerate any human pretensions to equality with him.'[73] In the Babel story we see a tragic example of how the gift of creativity, given to humanity in order to enable us to represent the creator, has thus been turned on its head. God had given us the ability to build order into creation, 'but when people are disobedient to God the intended order begins to disintegrate because the whole creation is influenced by human behaviour.'[74] So at the Fall, Adam and his descendants did not lose God's image but they did lose their intimate relationship with God which was necessary for humanity to remain fully human. We will now see that a further result was that the image was marred in such a way as to frustrate and compromise God's calling to mankind to be labourers, with him, in the task of stewarding creation.

The Fall and Human Dominion

If the image of God does not just consist of a relational dimension but also possesses a functional component which expresses itself in the task of godly dominion, we also need to ask what happened to the expectation that we were to steward the earth towards wholeness and fruitfulness. Does our now tarnished image mean that we are no longer capable of fulfilling our responsibilities to care for the earth? And if so, is it a calling that we are still expected to honour, or has it become too far out of our reach to remain realistic? These questions are important, because if humans forfeited dominion through the Fall, Alexandre Ganoczy is right in saying that the ecological scope of the Christian hope is markedly reduced and replaced 'with an individual-ethical ascetic perspective.'[75] If, on the other hand, we continue to possess God's image and calling, the future remains 'ecologically open. Even fallen human beings can and should rule in terms of the task entrusted to them by creation.'[76]

The answer to this question seems to be that despite the breakdown in relationships wrought by the Fall it has not 'substantially effected our duties. What it did, rather, was to make the performance of those duties more onerous.'[77] This is made very clear in Genesis 9 where the writer repeats the dominion statement of Genesis 1; although with one very important addition:

> Be fruitful and increase in number and fill the earth. The fear and dread of you will fall upon all the beasts of the earth, and all the birds of the air, upon every creature that moves upon the ground, and upon the fish of the sea; they are given into your

hands. Everything that lives and moves will be food for you. Just as I gave you the green plants, I now give you everything.[78]

The change to this new dominion statement is seen in the recognition that creation's estimate of its rulers is now defined by the words 'fear' and 'dread'. 'This is alienation as seen from the non-human side of creation.'[79] Just as it was significant that the first moral test of our obedience affected our relationship with the natural order[80] so the fact that the result of Adam's disobedience is seen in the straining of that relationship is also very meaningful. So our sin is not only rebellion; 'but it is also refusal to accept the true constituted nature of the universe of which man is part.'[81]

The bible makes a great deal of the link between human sin and natural disorder. From the indication that it is Cain's murder of Abel that results in the ground no longer yielding its crop,[82] through the events of the flood[83] and Hosea's insistence that sin results in the mourning of the land and even in reversals of creation[84] and finally to Paul's graphic account of the groanings of creation waiting for liberation; the scriptural witness emphatically affirms a link between sin and ecological disharmony. This can either be seen as God allowing the natural order to violate humanity in return for our violation of it or it can be understood as God detailing what the natural effects of our unwise and exploitative behaviour will be. But the relationship is not limited to bad effects. Just as judgement brings (or is seen in) a resultant degree of disorder, the bible writers also equate promised blessing with obedience.[85] Since post-Fall creation is given the hope that we might still be able to bring blessings upon ourselves and creation through the right exercise of human dominion, this must imply that correct choices are still possible today.

Perhaps the most potent symbol of the disharmony between us and nature is seen in the second addition to the dominion statement in Genesis chapter 9. At the dawn of creation the

Genesis account suggests that humans were created to be vegetarians; now we are pitted against bird, fish and animal and are permitted to kill them for food. It is as if we take it upon ourselves to add to the definition we were encouraged to give the animals in 2:19; and they can now be classified according to whether or not they are good for food. The relationship between us and the animals has clearly undergone a fundamental change. It might be too strong to say that animals were not previously intended for human use since this is an argument from silence; but it is certainly the case that their fear and dread are well founded, since the well-being of the animal kingdom is now a practical consideration only in so far as their survival is the only way we can be ensured of a plentiful supply of meat. I am not sure whether in fact it is possible to make a choice between the idea that God uses the natural order to punish us and the suggestion that linking sin to environmental devastation is God's way of illustrating an effect whose cause is revealed as our ongoing sinful behaviour. However the fact is that God now allows us to intervene in creation in deadly ways;[86] and there can be no doubt that the linking of fear and dread with God's acceptance that man and animal will now kill each other – out of fear as well as for food – is the most striking symbol the Genesis writer gives us as to the fundamental change in the relationship between humans and nature.

But are we to see this change as sanctioning other exploitative attitudes and actions? And does this mean that a fallen, and possibly hostile, world will now only respond to violent methods of control? Harvey Cox believes the Fall 'disenchanted' nature and turned it into a secular entity[87] whilst Robert Whelan suggests that Christians should view nature as something against which it is impossible to sin.[88] But to think this way is to confuse description with prescription. To be sure, Genesis 9 describes a world in which our dominion over nature has become the kind of control that instils fear and dread, but this does not mean that it is teaching us that we are entitled to act in this way. As Ron Elsdon says:

> To argue in this way is parallel to taking Jesus' words 'you will always have the poor with you' as justifying the existence and perpetuation of poverty. Genesis is a divine statement about human inability to control the environment properly, even though the responsibility of dominion has not been removed; it does not suggest that violence is to be encouraged.[89]

I conclude that 'humans indirectly bring about environmental destruction as the outcome of sin, or do so directly through their foolish arrogance.'[90] and that despite the difficulties imposed by the Fall, and our broken relationship with both the creator and our created environment; we are still called to uphold and respect our covenant relationship with God and act as just and wise stewards of creation.

The Fall and Nature

So in Genesis 3, the writer shows how the Fall fractures relationships between creator and mankind. But the text also reveals evidence of a wider breakdown. Tim Marks helps us identify the full implications of the Fall when he writes:

> If we look at the problem of sin in personalist terms we might say that sin has broken down five sorts of relationships, the repairing and renewing of which give us the agenda of Christ's kingdom.[91]

He explains first how Genesis 3 describes an alienation between each person and God; us and our fellow human beings; and within ourselves. But then verse 17 onwards describes how Adam's disobedience also had a knock-on effect upon the rest of creation. The earth now produces weeds and thistles and no longer freely yields the fruit it once did. This then is the fourth broken relationship, but there is a fifth which 'does not so much affect man as God.'[92] The earth was made in order to be offered up to God in worship and wholeness. And God's intention was to bless and sustain creation through us – his co-creators. The final result of the Fall has therefore been to place a gulf between God and his creation. This separation from its creator subjects it to frustration, and since its usurpers are themselves subject to the limitations and frustrations of that same fractured relationship they both groan together, waiting for liberation.[93]

But if I were to stop at this point and conclude this section on the Fall here, I would be recounting only half a story, and be guilty of extreme human centredness into the bargain. When we reach the point in God's judgement at which the ground is cursed, some vital questions emerge which are, as yet, unanswered.

In Hebrew thought a spoken curse was considered to be 'an active agent for hurt.'[94] Are we to understand this hurt as being directed at the nature of the soil itself, or was it directed at the purpose for which the soil was made? To put it another way, 'Is the earth "fallen" or is it as it was created to be?' I believe there to be three possible options.

The first is that the material creation was good until Adam's disobedience, at which point it became intrinsically marred. This indeed is the most common way of interpreting the phrase 'cursed is the ground because of you' in Genesis 3:17, since many commentators see it as suggesting that the Fall produced actual changes in the ground itself, and in both the pathology and physiology of plants and animals. Thus these verses are believed to describe how the natural order is in itself, not just how it is in regard to us. The strongest attraction of this view is moral; since it enables us to blame ourselves for the 'evils' of nature rather than God. Augustine seems to favour this interpretation when, in writing against the Pelagian heretics he pointed to nature's failings, and deduced that they were proof that it had been corrupted by the sin of Adam.[95] Whilst we might agree with Augustine that some of the human experience of life is indeed ugly, unpleasant and unhappy, we have already seen that God indicates that human obedience can still bring blessing, and neither has he rescinded his command that the earth should give forth its fruit. Surely Augustine is being too negative about the world in which we live, and human experience is incompatible with an intrinsically marred creation. In any case, Genesis 3 talks about an expulsion from Eden, not a metaphysical change within the garden itself. As Arthur Lewis observes:

> Nothing in the narrative suggests that the realm of nature has been altered in a fundamental way ... There is no indication that the Lord God added thorns to the roses or sharp teeth to the carnivorous animals.[96]

The second possibility is that our sin affected the future of the universe and also, somehow, affected its past. Thus Adam and Eve, whilst they were in the garden of Eden, were ignorant of the state of the outside world, but when they were banished from the garden, found themselves in the world as we now know it. But if they had not rebelled, maybe they would have discovered a different, unfallen, world outside Eden. The problem with this is that it suggests that an effect can precede a cause without appealing to any evidence that this could be so.

The third possibility is suggested by theologians like Alvin Plantinga, N.P. Williams, and C.S. Lewis,[97] who argue that creation shows the marks of a pre-Adamic 'cosmic' Fall. C.S. Lewis says:

> It seems to me ... a reasonable supposition, that some mighty created power had already been at work for ill on the material universe ... before ever man came on the scene ... If there is such a power, as I myself believe, it may well have corrupted the animal creation before man appeared.[98]

This, like the previous hypotheses, is based upon a recognition that our world is full of death, disease and suffering, and the assumption that it therefore cannot, as it stands, be creation as God intended and planned it. The point at which it departs from these views is in its insistence that neither can the earth's extreme fallenness be the sole responsibility of humanity. The present state of things must mean that either some external agent(s) corrupted the universe, or that the universe itself is in rebellion against God.

Plantinga notes that that his idea appeals to a much neglected aspect of Christian tradition extensively used by Augustine who:

> attributes much of the evil we find to Satan or to Satan and his cohorts. Satan, so the traditional doctrine goes, is a mighty non-human spirit, who along with many other angels, was created long before God created man. Unlike most of his colleagues, Satan rebelled against God and has been wreaking whatever havoc he can. The result is natural evil. So the natural evil we find is due to the free actions of non-human spirits.[99]

Stephen Davis concedes that this theodicy seems offensive to those who find it impossible to conceive of a truly evil satanic being. But, he insists, 'truth is not decided by a majority vote'.[100] My initial feeling about this view was that I found it attractive to think of a creation that had been distorted prior to human arrival because it seemed to me that natural evil was an unfairly large burden to place upon human shoulders. It also helped explain why natural evil pre-dates the human race. My problem was that I could not find anything in the creation story to imply any spoiling of nature by Satan – or any other 'angelic' being. And given that in Genesis God pronounces judgement upon the snake, and in Job Satan has to be given permission before he can act against Job, his family and his livestock, it was hard to conceive that

Satan would have the power or authority to carry out such a destructive act.

But, on further reflection, it became clear that there is nothing in the creation story that explains the snake's desire to thwart God. The very existence of the snake implies that there is some kind of enemy of God existing prior to Genesis 3. If, as Dom Illtyd Trethowan says, sin started with angels who exercised their free will, refused to accept grace and proudly resisted and rebelled against God[101], it would provide a way of attributing the whole realm of evil to the actions of created beings, would describe how the entry of evil into the universe preceded humanity, and would also make it easier to understand passages such as Genesis 6:1-4.

It seems possible then that after some kind of angelic rebellion, the earth went through a dislocation – possibly because these angelic beings were assigned some sort of stewarding role which they were then unwilling to fulfil. Then, instead of becoming part of the creator's intended solution:

> human beings compounded the problem by themselves rebelling. Genesis 3 can thereby hold humanity responsible for the divisions ... [between themselves and] creation, without requiring that no such divisions existed prior to the Fall.[102]

I therefore posit the possibility that the earth – at least outside Eden – underwent some kind of fall prior to the creation of humanity, and that God's comments in Genesis 3:17-19 refer to the fact that he created Adam and Eve to subdue the suffering and pain which had already distorted his good world, but because of their rebellion the earth was destined to remain in its frustrated state. Through all this, we humans remain responsible for our part in the Fall and also retain our responsibility to exercise just stewardship; whilst the earth remains an 'innocent' victim – a fact which the writer of Jonah seems to confirm when he writes of God telling the prophet Jonah that the animals in the city of Nineveh are 'innocent' and, along with the children, are not deserving of the punishment he threatens to bring upon the city's sinful inhabitants.[103] Before the Fall, Eden seems to have been an ideal home – even though it needed subduing and ruling. There is no indication that the land outside Eden was in the same state. This new home presented Adam and Eve with new challenges, primarily because it was not as easy to farm as Eden had been.

If Genesis 3:17-19 does not teach us that these plants (and, by extension, animals, forests etc.) which get in the way only do so because of our sin, there is less room created for the temptation that we can thus do what we like with whatever gets in the way of our progress. This is important since:

> our own time has shown us painfully [that] there are very few plants which we are not capable of regarding as weeds, and the same is true of animals, hills, valleys – indeed most things in creation. The ground is cursed because we are set against it.[104]

We have already noted the play on words between Adam and *adama*, and after asserting that this is the writer's way of describing a division within Adam himself, Wilkinson goes on to say that:

> division is man's own inability to be at harmony with the earth – his tendency to regard his difference with nature as enmity with nature. In short, the curse describes not a quality in the earth itself, but a human misuse of dominion. An accurate reading of the Hebrew word would be 'cursed is the ground to you.'[105]

We have to move on to the New Testament – to Romans 8 – to find the most explicit discussion of this wider aspect of the Fall.

> For the creation was subjected to frustration, not by its own

choice, but by the will of the one who subjected it, in hope that the creation itself will be liberated from its bondage to decay and brought into the glorious freedom of the children of God. We know that the whole creation has been groaning as in the pains of childbirth right up to the present time. Not only so, but we ourselves, who have the firstfruits of the Spirit, groan inwardly as we wait eagerly for our adoption as sons, the redemption of our bodies.[106]

In this passage Paul is personifying nature – which, according to Cranfield, he understands as the sum total of animate and inanimate nature.[107] The first thing that becomes clear is that it is the whole universe that suffers under the effects of the Fall, and that same universe currently longs for liberation in much the same way as its human inhabitants do.[108] And yet, earlier in his letter, Paul also states:

For since the creation of the world God's invisible qualities – his eternal power and divine nature – have been clearly seen, being understood from what has been made, so that men are without excuse.[109]

At first glance, these verses seem to contradict each other. On the one hand we read of Paul's supreme confidence that the whole earth clearly displays God's goodness, and then on the other we note that this same creation is 'in bondage to decay,' and eagerly waits to be set free at some point in the future. But need there be a tension here?

The difficulty is that although Paul shows that nature did not remain intact (Romans 8:20) he gives no indication of either the extent or, above all, the form of the change.[110] We know that we no longer live in a perfect garden. But the Psalms sing of the glory of the creation we inhabit, Job celebrates its majestic power and wonder and Jonah declares it to be innocent. I have to agree with Wilkinson's comments on Genesis 3 – that the Fall primarily affects our *relationship* with the natural world. But this does not deny the fact that the earth has undergone some kind of radical change – for to say otherwise would contradict the Genesis story. We cannot escape the fact that, in some way, the earth fell because we fell; and that we are responsible for its fallenness. The changes to both mankind and the earth have also made it harder for us to understand and appreciate the planet God has given us. Cranfield supports this idea when he says that this world is 'subjected to the frustration of not being able to fulfil the purpose of its existence, God having appointed that without man it should not be made perfect.'[111]

Perhaps the most important question to ask at this point is 'who was it that subjected the creation to this frustration in the first place?' The traditional understanding – where the question is discussed – is that it was inflicted by God himself. Consequently a number of translators of this passage give the word 'him' a capital letter. But need this be the case? Looking at the alternatives, we can discount the possibility that the 'one who subjected it' was Satan for reasons already stated – although I do believe that behind Romans 1:20 we can see an indication of the spiritual agenda of the forces of evil, whereby tempting and encouraging us to ravage creation in turn has the (intended) effect of making 'God's eternal power and divine nature' less clearly seen. In this respect, God really does suffer when his creation is violated. Another possibility is that perhaps it is we who are responsible for subjecting creation to its frustration since it was Adam's sin which began the Fall. Ganoczy writes. 'Who has enslaved it? Who has so 'subjected it', this creation . . . that is now in need of liberation? We human beings have.'[112] Henri Blocher expresses agreement with this view due to the parallels he sees between this passage and Genesis 3:17. What is more, he insists, 'that would fit with what follows: it is the redemption of man that will bring with it the redemption of the cosmos, just as his Fall affected the world.'[113]

It is crystal clear that it is we who must take the blame for creation's frustration. Thus the word 'frustration' (*mataioteti*) is best understood as teaching us that the Fall produced a dislocation of God's plans for the development of the cosmos. Instead of the purposeful unfolding of creation we see futility and (as the Good News bible translates it) a loss of purpose. But it cannot be us who *subjected* creation to its frustration. The subjector has to be God since only he could subject it 'in hope'; and the omission of a definite subject to the statement makes it probable that Paul is using a 'Divine Passive' tense.[114] But in reaching this conclusion we must be careful to avoid the implication that God deliberately subjected animals to pain and cruel treatment by humans out of a blatant disregard for nature. This is firstly because it is impossible to reconcile this with even the most primitive concepts of justice. Still less does it resonate with what Jesus himself said about God's care for (in this instance) the birds.[115] Secondly, the idea that God should treat nature in such an uncaring fashion contradicts the discoveries we made in the first part of this study. The fact that nature is not 'fallen' in the same way as we are is also important because if it were, and that fallenness produced a wilderness which refused to be tamed, we would be forced to sympathize with those who believe that the only way to work with nature is to dominate and plunder it. Again it seems that a creation which has been frustrated by the creator as a result of our disobedience is used by God as a tool of punishment and as a constant reminder of the extent to which things are so fundamentally wrong.

We have now caught a glimpse of harmony within the created order, and also concluded that the disruption to this harmony was brought about by human sin, and affected the whole of the created order – primarily due to the fact that every relationship within creation has been disrupted. I now want to look at God's response to this state of affairs. The next chapter examines God's response revealed in the rest of the Old Testament – rooted in the covenant and demonstrated in the law, the prophets and the Old Testament wisdom literature. I will also be exploring the reason why humanity possesses the image of God and will consider what God's injunction to us to 'rule' and 'subdue' the earth really means. The final chapter will look at the promise of redemption that comes with the arrival of the promised Messiah and the rule of the Kingdom of God.

Notes

1. Robert Johnston. – 'Wisdom Literature and its Contribution to a Biblical Environmental Ethic.' in Wesley Granberg-Michaelson (ed.) – *Tending the Garden.* op. cit. p 82.
2. H. Paul Santmire – 'Reflections on the Alleged Ecological Bankruptcy of Western Theology.' in *The Anglican Theological Review.* April 1975. Vol. 57. No 2.
3. H. Paul Santmire – *The Travail of Nature. The ambiguous Ecological promises of Christian Theology.* (Fortress. Philadelphia, Pennsylvania. 1985)
4. Santmire uses the term 'the-anthropological' which he admits to borrowing from Karl Barth. Santmire. op. cit. (1975). pp 133-135.
5. Ibid. p 135-6.
6. Ibid. p 143-4.
7. F.B. Welbourn - 'Man's Dominion.' *Theology.* Vol. LXXVIII. November 1975. No 655. p 567-8. Welbourn also refers – albeit in passing – to the fact that another of the 'fascinating products of the time was the attempt to derive atomism from Moses'.
8. See Chris Park – *Caring for Creation.* (Marshalls. London. 1992) p 102-3, and the references he cites there.
9. A.R. Peacocke – 'On the Historical Roots of our Ecological Crisis.' in Hugh Montefiore (ed.) – *Man and Nature.* (Collins London 1975) op. cit. p 156, and John Passmore – *Man's Responsibility for Nature: Ecological problems and Western Traditions.* (Scribner. New York. 1974) p 26.
10. Ibid. p 104.
11. Welbourn. op. cit. (1975) p 568.
12. Santmire. op. cit. (1975) p 133.
13. Lynn White Jr. – 'The Historical Roots of our Ecologic Crisis.' (*Science* 10 March 1967. Vol 155 No 3767) p1206.
14. Romans 7:14-24.
15. Montefiore. op. cit. (1975)
16. Matthew Fox – *The Coming of the Cosmic Christ.* (Harper & Row. New York. 1988) p 48.

17. John Millbank – 'Out of the Greenhouse.' in *New Blackfriars*. (Oxford. January 1993) p 10.
18. See J. S. Hurst – 'Towards a Theology of Conservation.' in *Theology*. April 1972. No. 622. Vol. LXXV. p 198-9.
19. Montefiore. op. cit. (1975) p 36.
20. Mary Baker Eddy – *Science and Health with Key to the scriptures*. (First Church of Christ the Scientist. Boston, Mass. 1971) pp 395, 585.
21. Millard Erickson – *Christian Theology*. (Marshall Morgan and Scott. Basingstoke. 1987) p 418.
22. J. Cobb and D. Griffin – *Process Theology: An Introductory Exposition*. (Westminster Press, 1976) p 52.
23. Ruth Page – *God and the Web of Creation*. (SCM Press. 1996) p 101.
24. See William Dumbrell – *Covenant and Creation. An Old Testament Covenantal Theology*. (Paternoster. Exeter. 1984) pp 33-39 and Blocher – 'In the Beginning.' op. cit. p 135-6.
25. Hosea 6:7.
26. Gerhard von Rad – *Genesis*. (SCM. London. 1972) p 82.
27. Genesis 2:19.
28. Von Rad. op. cit. p 87.
29. Blocher. *In the Beginning* (IVP. Leicester. 1984) p 142.
30. Ibid.
31. Claus Westermann – *Genesis 1-11*. (SPCK. London. 1984) pp 239, 256.
32. Blocher. op. cit. (1984) p 140.
33. This is a literal translation of Genesis 3:4.
34. Blocher. op cit. (1984) p 139.
35. Westermann. op. cit. (1974) p 93.
36. Elsdon – *Greenhouse Theology*. (Monarch. Speldhunt, Kent. 1992) p 82.
37. Von Rad. op. cit. (1972) p 81.
38. Ibid. p 89.
39. Blocher. op. cit. (1984) p 140-1.
40. Von Rad. op. cit. (1972) p 90.
41. Westermann. op. cit. (1984) p 249.
42. Genesis 3:17 and Romans 5:12-19.
43. Westermann. op. cit. (1984) p 250.
44. Genesis 2:25.
45. Tim Marks – *His Light in Our Darkness*. (Kingsway. Eastbourne. 1988) p 48-9.
46. Blocher. op. cit. (1984) p 173.
47. See Isaiah 65:25; Micah 7:17.
48. Von Rad. op. cit. (1972) p 92.
49. Westermann. op. cit. (1984) p 260-1 and *Creation*. op. cit. (1974) p 100.
50. See Romans 16:20.
51. Blocher. op. cit. p 180.
52. See von Rad. op. cit. (1972) p 93 and Westermann. (1984) op. cit. p 262.

53. See Genesis 4:7 and Song of Songs 7:10.

54. Genesis 3:20.

55. Westermann. op. cit. (1984) p 263.

56. Again, there is no reason why we should see the roles as they are represented here as being prescriptive. They simply reflect and describe the society in which they were composed.

57. Von Rad. op. cit. (1972) p 94.

58. Genesis 2:15.

59. Hosea 10:8 and Matthew 13:24-30 contain the same ideas. Hosea uses the same words as the Genesis writer when he says 'Thorns and thistles will grow up and cover their altars.' This points to the overwhelming and dominating nature of the weeds.

60. Romans 5:12ff.

61. Genesis 5:24 and 2 Kings 2:11.

62. Westermann. op. cit. (1984) p 267.

63. Von Rad. op. cit. (1972) p 95.

64. Blocher. op. cit. (1984) p 184.

65. See Romans 5:12-21 and 1 Corinthians 15:21.

66. Moss – *The Earth in our Hands*. (IVP. Leicester. 1982) p 55.

67. Blocher. op. cit. (1984) p 187. See also Psalm 82.6f and Ezekiel 28:9, 16f.

68. Genesis 5:1-3; 9:5-6; 1 Corinthians 11:7; James 3:9.

69. e.g. Colossians 3:10-11.

70. Sherrard. *The Rape of Man and Nature* (Golgonooza Press. 1987) op. cit. p 44.

71. Larry Rasmussen – 'Returning to our Senses. The Theology of the Cross as a Theology for Eco-Justice.' in Dieter Hessel. (ed.) – *After Nature's Revolt. Eco-Justice and Theology*. op. cit. p 52.

72. Genesis 11.

73. Welbourn. Man's Dominion (*Theology* Vol. LXXVIII Nov 1975) p 563.

74. John Biggs – 'Order and Chaos.' *Theology Themes*. (Northern Baptist College. Manchester. Spring 1992) p 7.

75. Alexandre Ganoczy – 'Ecological Perspectives in the Ecological Doctrine of Creation.' *Concilium*. 1991-4. (SCM Press. ed. Johann Baptist Metz & Edward Schillebeeckz.) p 47.

76. Ibid.

77. Passmore – *Man's Responsibility for Nature*. op cit. p 6.

78. Genesis 9:1-3. See also Psalm 8 & Hebrews 2:5-9.

79. Ron Elsdon. *Greenhouse Theology. Biblical Perspectives on Caring for Creation*. (Monarch. Speldhurst, Kent.) 1992 p 80.

80. Genesis 2:17 and 3:6.

81. Rowland Moss – 'The Ethical Underpinnings of Man's Management of Nature.' *Faith and Thought*. vol. iii No 1. (1985) p 41.

82. Genesis 4:10-14.

83. Genesis 7-9.

84. Hosea 4:1-3.
85. e.g. Genesis 26:12; Psalm 67:6-7 etc.
86. Although even this intervention has limits which are intended to ensure man's continued appreciation of the sacredness of life – Genesis 9:4-6; Leviticus 7.27; 17:11.
87. Harvey Cox – *The Secular City.* op. cit. p 23-4.
88. Whelan – *Mounting Greenery.* (IEA. London. 1989) op. cit. p 57.
89. Elsdon. op. cit. p 80.
90. Jeanne Kay. Concepts of Nature in the Hebrew Bible *Environmental Ethics)* Winter 1988 Vol 10 p 320.
91. Tim Marks – 'Wholeness.' *Evangel magazine.* (Summer 1989). p 5.
92. Ibid. p 7.
93. Romans 8.20-23.
94. Article by J. Motyer on The Fall. *New Bible Dictionary.* 2nd edition. (IVP. Leicester. 1982.)
95. Augustine – *Opus Imperfectum Contra Julianum.* 6, 27.
96. Arthur Lewis – 'The Localisation of the Garden of Eden.' *BETS* 11. (1968) p 174.
97. See Alvin Plantinga – *God, Freedom and Evil.* (Eerdmans. Grand Rapids, Michigan. 1974); C.S. Lewis – The Problem of Pain. (The Centenary Press. London. 1941) and N. P. Williams – *The Ideas of the Fall and of Original Sin.* (1927).
98. C.S. Lewis. op. cit (1941) p 122-123.
99. Alvin Plantinga. op. cit (1974)
100. Stephen Davis (ed.) *Encountering Evil: Live options in Theodicy.* (T&T Clark. Edinburgh. 1981) p 75.
101. Dom Illtyd Trethowan – An Essay in Christian Theology. (Longmans. London. 1954) p 128.
102. Michael Lloyd – 'Fall' in *Dictionary of Ethics, Theology and Society.* (Routledge. 1996) p 370.
103. Jonah 4:11.
104. Loren Wilkinson – *Earthkeeping in the Nineties.* (Eerdmans. Grand Rapids Michigan. 1992) p 290.
105. Ibid.
106. Romans 8:20-23.
107. C.E.B. Cranfield – *Romans. A Shorter Commentary.* (Eerdmans. Grand Rapids, Michigan. 1985) p 194.
108. Compare Romans 8:19 with verse 23.
109. Romans 1:20.
110. Blocher. op. cit. (1984) p 183.
111. Cranfield. op. cit. (1985) p 196.
112. Ganoczy. op. cit. p 44.
113. Blocher. op. cit. (1984) p 183 (footnote 26).

114. John Ziesler – *Paul's Letter to the Romans.* TPI New Testament Commentary. (SCM. London. 1989) p 220.
115. Matthew 6:26.

CHAPTER THREE

~

God's Covenant with Creation

Humanity and Nature

Lynn White's seminal article is centred around two main theses. The first is that it is the fusion of the brains of modern science with the brawn of technology which has produced the means by which the West has been able rapidly to increase the sum of human creature comforts in this last century. In order for this distinctly Western phenomenon to happen, an industrial monster was created which viewed nature as something to be conquered and used to satisfy human greed. To that end the non-human world was ravaged and despoiled. The second thesis is that since Western society has uniquely Christian roots, White believes it is natural to suppose that the Christian religion should take part of the blame for being a catalyst for this chain of events. White asserts that Christianity is the most human centred world religion, and as such it has replaced traditional animist reverence for nature with its own brand of arrogant domination. As if to illustrate his case White states that every major scientist in the medieval period was motivated by his Christian faith and often regarded himself more as a theologian than a scientist.

Without doubt Lynn White is correct in his assertion that the Christian Church has, throughout its history, contained a number of theologians who have taught a low view of nature. So we read that Origen, writing in the third century, argues against the pagan Celsus stating 'even the wildest of animals . . . were made for the exercise of our rational being.'[1] Augustine later betrays the neo-Platonist ideas of his religious past when he wrote in *Soliloquies*, 'These things of the senses are to be utterly shunned and the utmost care must be used lest while we bear this body our wings be impeded by their snare.'[2]

This thinking seems to be carried forward to the medieval period and beyond, for when we come to the seventeenth century and examine the beliefs of those scientists White mentions, his case continues to remain strong. In 1597 Francis Bacon proclaimed 'Knowledge itself is power'[3] and later wrote 'the empire of man over things depends wholly upon the arts and sciences.'[4] By his own admission, Bacon's actions were motivated by the belief that through the gift of science God had presented humanity with the means to regain the rightful dominion over the animals which he believed had been lost at the Fall. John Passmore traces the thread of thought from Bacon, through Descartes, Darwin, Spencer, Marx and Engels; and reaches the conclusion that 'their [Bacon and Descartes] interpretation was absorbed into the ideology of modern Western societies, Communist as well as Capitalist, and has been exported to the East.'[5]

Thus, whilst White's historical observations are accurate, I believe the weakness of his thesis is to be found in his understanding of cause and effect. This is most notable in his acceptance that a person's actions *must* be in accord with, and stem from, his own beliefs. It is simply not enough to spot someone who claims a Christian faith and then assume that *all* his actions will arise from and be determined by his beliefs. We must allow for misunderstanding and a degree of discontinuity, both on the part of the church at the time and the individuals concerned. In addition to this, we must be wise enough to recognize the tendency of fallen human beings to read into their religion the teachings they want to find there – especially when such scientists were driven by the excitement of new technological innovations which contained such tremendous possibilities for increased knowledge and power.

I also want to question White's assumption that these scientists' understanding of biblical teachings is orthodox.

Passmore indicates that Origen's teachings on nature were, as we might suppose, from Stoic roots and therefore do not have a Hebraic-Christian background.[6] What is more, although we may want to criticize these teachings of Origen and Aristotle (and others!) for their human centredness we must acknowledge that they do not actually denigrate creation or advocate its ill-treatment. Their main focus of attention is the salvation of the human soul, and whilst I would argue that this goal reflects their limited Platonic perspective on what is truly human, it is important to note that they only imply that nature is of no value *in this regard alone*. In fact there is evidence to indicate that these early fathers of the church had a great respect for and appreciation of nature. It is only possible to understand the perspective of the Early Church Fathers when we recall the particular issues they were concerned to address – often their works were provoked by specific heresies or the need for clear doctrine. The fact that they omitted to mention the place of nature does not therefore excuse the errors of the seventeenth century. And when we examine Bacon's view that humanity had power over nature in pre-Fall days this too is debatable, since it makes very human assumptions about the relationship between power and rule. Nowhere do the Hebrew scriptures indicate that the *'shalom'* (or wholeness and harmony) which pervades the pre-Fall account can be re-established by the use of dominant power. His idea that God has left mankind to achieve the ideal state by our own efforts is also questionable, and rings more of heretical Pelagianism than biblical Christianity.

Since it is the Genesis texts which have done so much to create and prolong the misunderstandings regarding the God-ordained relationship between humanity and nature[7] it is probably best if we begin this section there. It is at this point that we will pick up the thread we wove through the first chapter. We recall that mankind, created in the image of God, reflects his creator by being both in creation and over it in his position as ruler. The important point I derived from this was that, although the image of God has a substantive base, it is worked out in relationship and through the function of dominion-having.

If von Rad is correct when he says that less is said about the gift itself than about the task[8] it is only right that in this chapter we focus on the function of the image and upon any rules or boundaries which God puts on its working out.

The first result of being created in God's image is that humanity is entrusted with the task of ruling over the fish of the sea, the birds of the air, the livestock and all God's creation.[9] Verse 28 then tells mankind to subdue the earth. The Hebrew word for rule is *'radah'* and the word for subdue is *'kabas'*.

The Meaning of *Radah* and *Kabas*

The background of the verb *radah* comes from the imagery of treading down the wine press. It therefore means 'to trample' or 'subdue.'[10] Its use in Psalm 8 bears this out when the psalmist declares. 'You made him the ruler over the works of your hands; you put everything under his feet.'[11] The meaning of *kabas* is somewhat similar since it comes from a Hebrew word meaning 'to tread down,' 'bring into bondage,'[12] or 'stamp.'[13]

Given the roots of these words it is hardly surprising that aggressive interpretations of the injunction abounded until comparatively recent times. Lawrence Osborn comments that these images have given critics of Christian theology the idea that 'Christianity . . . gives divine sanction to rape the earth. In their eyes, dominion is merely a polite synonym for domination.'[14]

But James Barr disagrees with these critics when he points out that *radah* only has limited connections with the winepress, and concludes that its use here belongs to an entirely different 'semantic department'[15] in which it need not have a strong meaning. The word more often means 'rule' in the sense of 'govern' and is frequently found in the Old Testament in those passages which talk of kings ruling given areas – often in a peaceful way. William Dyrness agrees and insists that the fact the word has royal overtones means that the best method of interpretation is not found by examining what is meant *to us* by 'subdue' or 'trample,' or even what the terms meant in other nations at the same period in history. We will only find out what it means here by looking at the uniquely biblical concept of kingship.[16] When we do this, we discover that the biblical meaning of the word is somewhat different to its meaning in other cultures, since the biblical concept of rule found in the Old Testament describes activities undertaken by one who rules 'as a brother over brothers and sisters.'[17] In practice this meant that the king was forbidden to exploit his subjects or the earth since God demands that human rulership is in accord with the godly principles of justice and peace. So the ideal rule of a king in Israel implied no absolute right or authority, since the emphasis was on responsibility and servanthood. Thus we must beware lest we read secular understandings of ruling into the biblical records. The godly idea of rule is best seen in Philippians 2:7-11:

> Christ Jesus, who, being in very nature God,
> did not consider equality with God something to be grasped,
> but made himself nothing,
> taking the very nature of a servant,
> being made in human likeness.
> And being found in appearance as a man,
> he humbled himself
> and became obedient to death – even death on a cross.[18]

This is surely the understanding of kingship which should be read in here, with dominion being best expressed in terms of self-emptying rather than exploitation.[19] It is attentiveness to the world and consistent compassion that are the qualities God looks for, and produces, in the leaders of his people;[20] because, in doing so, they reflect God's nature and ensure just leadership.

So in Genesis 1:16 for example, the word *radah* clearly has a non-literal meaning. In verse 29 the God-given applications of ruling and subduing do not include the possibility of eating animals for food since this only became possible after the Fall. All this seems to indicate that the idea of dominion refers to the establishing of a creation order (not a hierarchy of value but of rule) and is certainly not a license for exploitation.

The word *kabas* in verse 28 is definitely a stronger word than *radah*, and it is used in four different, but related, ways. We first find it used (as here) of the land – for example, Canaan had to be subdued as Israel entered it.[21] It is then used of the subjugation of slaves,[22] forcible sexual domination,[23] and God's subduing of iniquity and the defeat of Israel's enemies.[24] Returning to its use here in Genesis, Barr notes that it is used in connection with the earth rather than the animals:

> I doubt whether more is intended here than the basic needs of settlement and agriculture. Man is to fill up the earth, take possession of it, and take control over it. Basically what is intended is tilling.[25]

The fact that a stronger word is applied to the land seems to lend support to the idea that the earth needed controlling in a way the animals did not – and this in turn seems to strengthen the case for the fall of the angels idea I preferred in the last chapter. If this is the case, humanity has been called to reimpose an order which was always God's intention for his creation but which was disrupted by the rebellion of part of it, and *kabas* describes the force which will be necessary if we are to be successful in our calling.

What is implicit in Genesis 1 becomes explicit as we look at what might be called a 'parallel passage' in chapter 2. In verse

15 the writer says. 'The Lord God took the man and put him in the Garden of Eden to work it and take care of it.' The Hebrew word for 'work' is *abad* and for 'take care' is *samar*.

The Meaning of *Abad* and *Samar*

The meaning of the verb *abad* parallels James Barr's translation of *radah*. It is the basic Hebrew word meaning 'serve' and in some places even reflects the idea of being a slave to that which is being served.[26] *Samar* implies a watchful care, and a command to preserve with a view to ensuring fruitfulness. The image is very close to that of a shepherd; which incidentally is also imagery the bible uses when referring to the rightful rule of kings.[27] The important thing to note about both these words is that the activities they encourage are for the sake of that which is being cared for rather than serving the needs of the carer. The cultural milieu is also such that the dominion these words imply could only have had a fairly restricted meaning since there was no potential for the kind of global impact that modern humanity can inflict. 'Most likely they would have understood dominion in terms of animal husbandry, cultivating the ground and developing culture.'[28]

Furthermore we see that the fruit of the earth is for the benefit of the animals as well as humans.[29] So, in a sense, we could say that we are serving the animals by tilling the earth and ensuring its continued productivity. But this does not mean that the vegetation only possesses a simple utilitarian value since the command to preserve the earth is followed by the exclamation 'it was very good;' a comment which affirms its true and inherent goodness.

Claus Westermann assures us that our task of dominion can only mean that a relationship with the creation is presupposed. He insists that since harmony is never achieved when we exterminate animals or remove species, but when we learn to live with or alongside them, it is in relationship that we learn what a blessing dominion can be. Furthermore, it is via relationship that animals have also been able to reciprocate in serving mankind. In this way true, biblical rulership opens the way for us to become genuinely human. It is hardly surprising that the blessings of partnership and harmony within creation are exactly what is promised to both human and beast as a result of obedience to God's commands.[30]

Perhaps it is in recognition that human and animal could live in a productive partnership together that God brings the animals to Adam in order to have him order and name them.[31] It must not be forgotten here that in the Hebrew culture the giving of names was a sign that the one doing the naming recognized the essential nature of that which was being named. Thus this passage illustrates that Adam sees something in each creature which suggests a name to him, which in turn somehow describes its function. Naming is a way of conferring status and meaning. It could also be argued that God is giving Adam the opportunity to see the goodness of creation in much the same way as he himself had done earlier – in which case, it is as if wise dominion is dependent upon an appreciation and understanding of the value of the gift as well as its purpose and potential.

But Adam is not only told to have dominion over the animals. God also directs him to till the earth so that it may produce all kinds of vegetation for him to eat. Chris Wright acknowledges that God provides a right of access to and use of the soil, but believes that the fact that men and women rule the earth in trusteeship under God means that:

> we are as responsible to God for what we do with what we produce as we are for what he has given us 'raw'. There is no mandate in the creation material for private *exclusive* use, nor for hoarding or consuming at the expense of others.[32]

The final thing to note here is that the notion of servanthood implies that someone must be master. Since it is impossible to believe that the bible teaches that the earth is the master of humanity, we are reminded that standing at the head of this newly designated order is the creator himself. Francis Schaeffer suggests that this whole section finds its New Testament parallel in the Parable of the Talents[33] in which God is acknowledged as the sovereign and rightful owner of all things, but entrusts them to his servants for wise and careful management.[34] It is interesting that in this story we also have mention of both rewards or blessings for correct behaviour, and punishments for disobedient and unwise stewardship. Santmire insists that as we begin to think holistically as opposed to self-centredly it becomes possible to think in terms of relationships that are co-operative and not exploitative. In order to do this it is necessary to think outside the usual parameters of either I-Thou or I-It relationships because neither is a suitable description of the way we are expected to view nature. Santmire suggests adding an *I-Ens* dimension where this relationship 'is a bonding of two beings from two different communities of being, one capable of personal communion and the other not.'[35]

In such a relationship the '*I*' contemplates the '*Ens*' as another creature with its own integrity before God and with its own value. The '*I*' never seeks to exploit the '*Ens*' and desires never to violate its integrity even though the '*I*' recognizes its difference. The '*Ens*' can never be property of the '*I*', since it always belongs to the creator; but instead the '*I*' is grateful to the creator for the '*Ens*'' existence. Once we see nature in this way, Santmire contends, it will be possible for us to become '*Homo cooperans*' – where we 'stand back and contemplate the "*Ens*" and see that it is good, and where "*Homo cooperans*" can then wait with humble and caring attention for opportunities to know and serve the "*Ens*".'[36] All this

> introduces us to a view of the universe and the human place in it
> that contains, in fact, a radical critique of every hierarchical

113

ordering of earthly life, every elevation of one species at the expense of others, and every attempt either to divinize or demonize the human creature.[37]

What we have seen so far is that God seems to have taken the initiative to work a set of relationships into the fabric of creation. God made us to relate to himself and govern nature whilst also being answerable to him. Nature relies on God for its sustenance, but it is through us that it is governed and managed. Harmony exists when these relationships are maintained, and blessing is the in-built result; but when relationships are neglected or fractured, disharmony is the natural conclusion. What we have then is a three-way relationship, initiated by God and maintained by adherence to a series of basic requirements. This is known as a covenant.

Covenant and Creation

The idea of Covenant is widely seen in scripture, and it simply denotes a binding agreement between two parties who are each obliged to keep their part of the bond. The Old Testament word for covenant is *berit* which is used to refer to a decision which is irrevocable, and covers a wide variety of agreements.[38] Most scholars agree that the word originally came from the non-Hebrew root *bara* which meant 'to bind.' In the Old Testament it is used to refer to a covenant between friends,[39] and rulers.[40] A more common occurrence is where one of the parties involved is much more powerful than the other – such as a king and his subjects.[41] In this case the more powerful party would impose the covenant upon those under him, and the weaker party would confirm their acceptance of the ordained rules in faith that the ruler was acting in the best interests of both parties.

It is this type of covenant in perpetuity (*berit olan*) which best describes the covenant adopted by God with his chosen people whom he brought out of captivity and into the freedom and security of covenant relationship.[42] Further examples of God's covenant with Israel are found with Noah after the flood,[43] with Abraham,[44] David[45] and with the whole people.[46] The important thing to notice here is that each new covenant does not displace or abrogate earlier ones. And each time God agrees to the same thing – to bind himself in covenant loyalty (*hesed*) and extend his love and grace to all who, by faith, are prepared to receive it and bind themselves to serve him in return. Sometimes previous covenants are clarified or made more specific, but with every restatement we see God declaring: 'I will be their God, and they will be my people.'[47] A feature of God's determination to bless his people is found in the fact that although each individual's place within the covenant is determined by his response in faith to God, the ultimate goal is one which God expresses his determination to fulfil. This is best seen in Genesis 12:2-3 where God mentions no conditional clauses and seven times he states his intention that the whole earth should know the creator's blessing. To this end we also note the establishment of a formal covenant renewal service[48] illustrating the endlessly forgiving nature of God, and his determination that the covenantal system of relationship should succeed.

The Beginning of the Covenant

It is usually assumed that the idea of covenant begins in Genesis 6 when, as God is preparing to destroy the earth by flood as punishment for the excessive wickedness he sees on it, he finds that Noah and his family are uncorrupted by the sin around them. It is at this point that he makes a covenant promise to save them.[49] After rescuing Noah and his family along with a stock of every species of creature upon the earth, God sees what he has done and promises to succeeding generations that he will never again destroy the earth by flood, gives the rainbow as a sign of this undertaking and restores the blessings of the early chapters of Genesis.[50]

Some scholars argue that although this is the first specific reference to a covenant, the restoration of the blessings upon the earth seems to look back 'to a divine relationship established by the fact of creation itself.' They argue this because in Genesis 6 there is an 'absence of the standard terminology of covenant initiation.'[51] Sean McDonagh cites Bernard Anderson, who notes the strong resemblance between Genesis chapters 1 and 9 and concludes that Genesis 9 is a restatement of what was the *original* covenant.[52] William Dumbrell agrees and says that Genesis 9 indicates

> that the covenant which was confirmed with Noah had been brought into existence by the act of creation itself...it is clearly not contingent upon human reaction to it or even dependant upon human knowledge of it. In the most general terms it proclaims the lordship of (humanity over) creation and care of the creator for what has been created.[54]

George Kehm adds that the

> Noachic covenant makes explicit and unambiguous the divine commitment to the preservation of creation that was only implicit and ambiguous in God's recognition of the original creation as 'very good'. God's commitment to the earth in the Noachic covenant may be taken as a sign of God's commitment to creation as a whole.[54]

Thus we can conclude that there is evidence to suggest that the covenant began with Adam, not Noah, and that it was stated more explicitly in Genesis 6, 9, 12 etc. because God saw the need to remind his people that the relationship between himself and mankind which was once a matter of course now depended both upon his faithfulness and his covenant love (*hesed*), and the obedience and humility of his people.

The Scope of the Covenant

Human pride might lead us to believe that the scope of the covenant is limited to God and humanity – indeed if we take Genesis 12 as our model this might be an acceptable conclusion. But God's covenant with Abraham must be seen in the context of his desire to establish a people whom he could bless, and through whom other nations could learn about God for themselves. But the covenant in Genesis 12 is only a sub-covenant of Genesis 9 (and, if I am correct above, Genesis 1); in which God does not restrict his covenant to mankind, but extends it *to the whole of creation.* So in Genesis 9:13 he describes the rainbow as 'the sign of the covenant between me and the earth.' 'I will remember my covenant between me and you and all living creatures of every kind' declares God in verse 15. 'Never again will the waters become a flood to destroy all life.' Then for added emphasis God repeats that the rainbow 'is the sign of the covenant I have established between me and all life on the earth.'

Working out the Covenant

The ultimate goal of the covenant is *shalom,* an ordered, secure relationship between God and his creation. At the heart of it is the faithfulness of God and his determination to bless the earth. However the reality is that all the explicit references to covenant in the bible come after the Fall, after which God does two things. The first is that he identifies himself with the weak, the poor and the oppressed. This recognizes that in a fallen world the language of domination and power speaks louder than any other, and so God expresses his determination that his will cannot be thwarted – at least in the long term – and he constantly reminds all who would seek to serve him of the central importance of righteousness and justice. The second thing we find is that the relationship between God and humanity which was once characterized by freedom to do anything but eat the fruit of a single tree is now governed by laws and regulations which are set in place in order to limit the reign of sin (presumably guarding the creation against the extreme excesses which led to the flood) and provide boundaries within which the blessing of God could still be found.

Thus in the law we see God's response to the Fall and the resulting 'disruption and degeneration of creation;'[55] and we notice the ongoing commitment of the creator to honour his covenant with creation. It is no surprise then that embedded deeply within the requirements of the law, the visions of the prophets and the reflections of the wisdom writers runs a thread of insistence that mankind care for the whole environment. It is to these sources that we now turn.

The Law of the Covenant
Possibly one of the most attractive features of the covenant as far as God's people were concerned is God's promise to bless them with their own land. This promise was first made to Abraham[56] and later repeated to Moses whom God also reminds: 'The whole earth is mine.'[57] Chris Park suggests that this promise, together with the directives which accompany it, offers us still more insight into how we should relate to nature in today's world, since land 'is a divine gift to fallen people.'[58] The fact that the whole earth belongs to God means that humanity has no claim to ownership of any part of it; but nevertheless is given charge over it and is permitted to share its fruit. This is becoming a familiar theme. The law suggests that we are best understood as tenants rather than freeholders because the gift is not permanent,[59] and, as landlord, God has laid down the rules which set out the nature of the tenancy and the requirements of the tenant. Within this role as landlord we also note that God recognizes his responsibility to care for the earth[60] and to ensure its continued fruitfulness in

accordance with his promises at the beginning.[61] Right treatment of the earth is also based upon an appreciation of the fact that God's gift is intended as an inheritance for future generations too. This understanding demands that its continued fruitfulness is also guarded and nurtured by its tenants, if only for the sake of their own future! To this end God gives the law.

At its heart, the law is an embodiment of pre-Fall principles which are set out in order that we can set our own standards correctly, and can be pointed to the God who offers forgiveness when we fail to meet his requirements.[62] The law also provides us with a set of guidelines and boundaries that embody the principles found in Genesis 1 and 2 and within which humanity can find God's blessing and can extend that blessing to their partners in creation. It is also the basis upon which the tenant will be held accountable to God for his actions.

It is hardly surprising that most of the law is concerned with Israel and its relationship with God, outsiders, and fellow Israelites. However, within this treatise for harmonious living we also find that a demand to treat the earth fairly and wisely surfaces at a number of points. The two major principles underlying these requirements are that the land belongs to God and that mankind are 'but aliens and my tenants;'[63] and God's concern that the earth continues to remain fruitful for future generations. Chris Park believes that these principles provide the basis for 'three most important rules' governing our dominion over creation.[64] These refer to destroying creation, the pain of animals and the restraint of the power of humanity.

I) Wanton Destruction
Deuteronomy 20 contains a set of rules governing acceptable behaviour in wartime. In verses 19 and 20 God declares: 'When you lay siege to a city . . . do not destroy its trees by putting an

axe to them, because you can eat their fruit. Do not cut them down. Are the trees of the field people, that you should beseige them?'

The Hebrew phrase used in this passage is *bal tashhit* which literally means 'do not wantonly destroy.' This suggests that in addition to their inherent value, the trees should be preserved out of respect for their instrumental fruit bearing potential. Park indicates that this passage was interpreted very widely by Jewish teachers and from it was derived prohibitions against all kinds of offences against men and nature.

II) The Treatment of Animals

In Leviticus and Deuteronomy we find a number of laws relating to the treatment of animals. Leviticus teaches the people of Israel not to take a young animal from its mother before it is seven days old,[65] whilst Deuteronomy insists that if a nest is discovered the mother bird is to be left untouched if the young birds are taken.[66] This law is presumably enforced in order to limit greed and ensure that whole species are not threatened. Deuteronomy also teaches that two animals of different strengths should not be harnessed together in order to protect the weaker animal,[67] and that an ox should be allowed to eat whilst it is treading out corn.[68] Underlying these three randomly distributed rules is an important principle that indicates a concern for the welfare of the various creatures mentioned. As a writer in Proverbs says. 'a righteous man cares for the needs of his animal, but the kindest acts of the wicked are cruel.'[69]

III) Land Management

Deuteronomy 8:18 affirms that it is God who gives humanity the ability to produce wealth, with the prophet Isaiah adding that wisdom regarding the correct treatment of the land comes from God who 'instructs him and teaches him the right way.'[70] Isaiah's words come in a passage in which he is comparing the wisdom of God to the disaster that results from disobedience. He is talking about farming methods and referring back to the law which insists that a pattern for sowing crops is important, both to ensure good yields and to preserve the land. So we read:

> For six years you are to sow your fields and harvest the crops, but during the seventh year let the land lie unploughed and unused. Then the poor among your people may get food from it, and the wild animals may eat what they leave. Do the same with your vineyard and your olive grove.[71]

> But in the seventh year the land is to have a sabbath of rest, a sabbath to the Lord. Do not sow your fields or prune your vineyards. Do not reap what grows of itself or harvest the grapes of your untended vines. The land is to have a year of rest. Whatever the land yields during the sabbath year will be food for you – for yourself, your manservant and maidservant, and the hired worker and temporary resident who live among you, as well as for your livestock and the wild animals in your land. Whatever the land produces may be eaten.[72]

These commands are clearly meant to place restrictions upon those for whom economic considerations outweigh ethical principles. This does not mean that God is unconcerned about the steady supply of food, for Leviticus indicates that God promises to reward obedience by ensuring that the land produces enough before the fallow year to store and eat during the year's break.[73] Instead, this restriction is intended to enable the people of God to enjoy the benefit of sabbath rest whilst remembering their dependence upon God. The sabbath is also important for the land. In fact it is so vital that God promises punishment to anyone who ignores the need for the land to have rest:

I will lay waste the land, so that your enemies who live there will be appalled . . . then the land will enjoy its sabbath years all the time that it lies desolate and you are in the country of your enemies . . . the land will have the rest it did not have during the sabbaths you lived in it.[74]

Exodus 23 extends the jubilee principle to the land and servants: 'six days do your work, but on the seventh day do not work, so that your ox and your donkey may rest and the slave born in your household, and the alien as well, may be refreshed.'[75]

Loren Wilkinson argues that this approach to land management is just as relevant and necessary today since these laws contain timeless wisdom and indicate certain God-ordained priorities. He shows how whenever humanity has 'harvested' the land in a way which respects its needs and refuses to exploit the soil it produced all that was required of it. However, where human 'wants' have driven us to farm the land intensively for short term benefit, the impact has often been disastrous whenever due attention has not been paid to natural balances. In *Earthkeeping in the Nineties* Wilkinson cites an example that relates specifically to the wisdom of land rest.[76] He shows how, out of a desire to produce 'ever more food with ever less labour' a monocrop system was developed throughout the USA. According to statistics produced for *Science* magazine[77] the result has been the gradual erosion and loss of topsoil, and a steady decrease in crop yield as a result. In order to maintain the capacity of the land to produce the required food more and more fertilizer has been needed. Fascinatingly, Wilkinson also includes details of American research that has shown that land is at its most productive (and continues to remain so) when a cycle is introduced whereby the it is allowed to remain fallow for two years in every five.

The Wisdom of the Covenant

The inherent wisdom of the law is compounded when we consider what is commonly known as the wisdom literature of the bible. According to Zimmerli, the wisdom tradition relates to the 'art of steering'[78] – meaning that it is most concerned about the knowledge which imparts wisdom to us as we seek to master our life. Thus, at its most fundamental level, wisdom is about the application of the laws we have just touched upon to everyday life. Von Rad suggests that:

> according to the convictions of the wise men, Yahweh obviously delegated to creation so much truth, indeed he was present in it in such a way that man reaches ethical *terra firma* when he learns to read these orders and adjusts his behaviour to the experiences gained.[79]

Since the wisdom writers focus on arguments which come from the experiences of life, it is not unrealistic to hope that they too might contribute some practical pointers which could help mankind fulfil the purposes for which he was created.

Our hope is rewarded when in Proverbs 8 we read the personified voice of wisdom proclaim:

> Does not wisdom call out?
> Does not understanding raise her voice?
> On the heights along the way, where the paths meet she takes her stand;
> beside the gates leading into the city, at the entrances, she cries aloud:
> 'To you O men I call out; I raise my voice to all mankind.
> You who are simple, gain prudence; you who are foolish, gain understanding.
> Listen, for I have worthy things to say; I open my lips to speak what is right . . .
> The Lord possessed me at the beginning of his work, before his deeds of old;

123

I was appointed from eternity, from the beginning, before the
world began . . .
Then I was the craftsman at his side.
I was filled with delight day after day, rejoicing always in his
presence,
rejoicing in his whole world and delighting in mankind.
Listen to my instruction and be wise; do not ignore it.'[80]

The first thing we note then is that godly wisdom is
concerned with that which Platonist wisdom would despise. It
reveals that the wise have learned that nature is valuable. It is
so important that Solomon, who was supposedly the wisest
man who ever lived, 'spoke three thousand proverbs . . . He
described plant life, from the cedar of Lebanon to the hyssop
that grows out of walls. He also taught about animals and birds,
reptiles and fish.'[81] It is interesting that of all the wise decisions
the writer could have mentioned, the most important feature
of Solomon's wisdom in this summary passage was his
knowledge and understanding of creation. What is more, he
does so without once making reference to its usefulness to
humanity.

Perhaps the most striking thing about the wisdom of
Solomon is that its goal was not the glorification of wisdom
itself, or even of the possessor of it. All biblical wisdom points
directly to God. Von Rad comments upon the easy adaptation
of the 'somewhat arid scientific material to the purposes of the
worship of Yahweh.'[82] Even the Queen of Sheba is forced to
acknowledge the wisdom of God who appointed and equipped
Solomon to fulfil his duties.[83]

The bible also indicates that the wisdom of Solomon related
to more than an ability to observe nature. He was presumably
also able to understand it and appreciate its complexity and
inter-relatedness. So Psalm 104, 'which has its source in the
wisdom materials of its day',[84] tells us about habitats and utters
praise of the ecologically wise ordering of creation. It is a Psalm

which praises the variety and mystery of creation, whilst also recognizing that God cares for it and sustains all he has made. It also paints a similar picture to the later chapters of Job,[85] informing us that everything has its meaning and purpose even if we are unable to understand it or make use of it ourselves.

After all, as we discovered earlier, creation does not exist simply for the purposes of humanity. This is perhaps most supremely illustrated in God's discourse to the complaining Job in which he issues a reminder that nature is arrayed without reference to him or his need, and that it is sustained by God's hand in places where he had never set foot.[86] John Austin Baker says that the contribution of the book of Job is to insist that the outlining of the wonders of creation uniquely serves:

> to make the point that humanity's whole attitude to the created order is wrong, because it is totally egoistic, totally anthropocentric. If humans were to stop even for a moment to consider the universe as it actually is, they would see that by far the greater part of it has no relevance to them at all. If God created behemoth and leviathan, it assuredly was not for humanity's benefit (chapters 40-41); it must have been for some purpose opaque to humans, who can think only in terms of themselves and their own situation. Such creatures glorify God in their existence according to rules far beyond our ken; God made them and delights in them for their own sake, not for some ulterior usefulness to us as human beings.[87]

The fact that God answers Job out of a whirlwind (which is a dust-bearing wind that can therefore be seen) is thought by Walter Gulick to be indicative of God's immanent presence with Job.[88] He further suggests that the whirlwind's tendency to turn all things around even shows that God is revealing to Job that it is his conceptions of him that have to change in this encounter. Whether or not this is the intended reason God appeared in the wind; Job is forced to rethink his theology. As he listens to God,

[Job] becomes a visionary, one who sees and understands . . . (Previously) God, the Lord of the Covenant, was known by hearing, by tradition; God, the Lord encountered in nature, is known by seeing, and this seeing leads to repentance and conversion.[89]

Job's conversion to a cosmological understanding of God persuades him that God not only reveals himself through nature, but his understanding and control of its immensity assures Job of its value and inherent goodness – putting his own problems and questions into perspective. The book of Job also reminds us that whatever the concept of dominion conjured up at the time of writing, it could only have had a fairly restricted meaning due to the limited technology available in these early societies.[90] In other words, humanity did not possess the capacity to destroy the earth, and the locus of our ability to dominate the earth did not extend far beyond taming the animals and cultivating the ground.

But it is not only in the specific references to nature that the wisdom writers speak to us. In fact their advice goes far deeper. Its greatest value is seen as we acknowledge that wisdom is rooted in reflected experience. It is certainly not law, but has a quality about it which helps the reader to appreciate the loving intent of the law. Put simply, the words we read in Ecclesiastes and Proverbs affirm that the law is wise. Its intention is to draw the reader in and invites him to experience the benefits of that wisdom for himself. So in Solomon's affirmation that the world looks to God not humanity for its sustenance, since it exists for him and reveals his glory and purpose; we are challenged to examine the beauty and order of creation and respect it and work with it when we exercise our dominion. Thus he calls us to observe with humility and let our understanding inform our behaviour.

The Demands of the Covenant

The law and the wisdom writers both set standards and encourage obedience. The prophet's role is in restoring wayward behaviour. In Amos, we see God challenging human complacency; and a firm corrective to the idea that God is simply concerned about the material progress of humanity. 'Israel's God is also the one who brings famine, blight, drought and mildew to warn his own people.'[91] So God also acts against his people where they persist in acting disobediently, and he sometimes does so by using nature as his tool.

Susan Gillingham believes that this has three implications. The first is that it underlines the fact that there is no barrier between God and nature. Secondly, it helps us to reconcile the themes of judgement and salvation, where judgement points to the hope of salvation. God himself embraces the chaos in order to set about the work of recreation. Finally, it shows how God works within creation and yet is still beyond it.

> God is more concerned with justice and righteousness than with the perpetuation of the rhythms of nature simply for the sake of complacent prosperity... A people who choose to live with violation around them will experience that same violation from the natural order, particularly when they live in the false belief that they have control over that order.[92]

The lesson here is that it is impossible to be living out of relationship with the creator and sustainer of all things, whilst at the same time expecting that the creation which owes its existence to him will be totally pliant to our desires.

Conclusion: Humanity as Stewards of Nature

My concern throughout this chapter has been to discover what the idea of covenant has to offer us as we search for theological insights which will help us to understand how and why we should care for the environment. At a number of places in our journey I have introduced the voice of Lynn White, who has not only been the catalyst for much of the work done in this area by Christians, but has also become the focal point around which critics of the faith have gathered. This is surprising since, as I mentioned in the introduction, White looks to Christian theology to play its part in righting the wrongs of recent centuries both by restating old teachings and by finding new ways to lead humanity towards a right treatment of the earth. I suggest that any decision about whether to agree with White's assertion that Christianity bears a burden of guilt for the despoliation of nature depends largely upon what evidence we are prepared to accept. There is certainly no doubt that the men he chooses to put in the dock are guilty of having a low view of nature and of turning dominion into domination. For some this was their stated intention. There is also probably enough evidence to suggest that the Christian faith has provided some of the essential foundation stones for the rise of modern science and technology. This in turn has provided mankind with the means to exert his influence. However the trial is not as simple as that, because, strictly speaking, Lynn White has not put the Christian Faith into the dock in his trial of individual Christians. The two are not synonymous.

When we looked at the creation story, three major themes became evident: the inherent goodness of creation, the fact that humans are created in the image of God, and the idea that this enables us to fulfil our intended dominion. We also discovered that at no place do the Hebrew scriptures reinforce the Platonic/Cartesian view of nature which has for so long been mistakenly thought of as Christian, and have attempted to provide a biblical response to the Greek idea that God is so utterly transcendent that he is not interested in matter. The God of the bible created the earth which he declared to be good, and came to earth as a *man* in order to *save all creation* from its bondage to decay.[93] Jürgen Moltmann argues against a

God who is self-sufficient and is therefore unaffected by anything in his creation when he insists that God's love is of the kind that is affected by the objects of his love. Thus he is sure that God is passionately concerned and vulnerably involved with his world.[94] We have also seen that God created us in his image so that we could have a relationship with him and represent him by tending the earth and ensuring its fruitfulness. This image of God is something unique to humanity and gives us the role of co-creators who have the function of mirroring the creator-God. Thus our dominion is to be *like* the dominion of God – concerned to bless and direct the creation towards wholeness. The indication is very much that we could be a blessing to creation if we chose right.[95]

> Here is the central drama of creation, in which the earth is fully involved. One almost has the impression that if this order is respected, the fruitfulness of the earth will be more or less a natural consequence. The implication is that the created order has more than a natural function; it also has an expressive or symbolic purpose that relates it to the purposes of God.[96]

Even though we live in a fallen world, and carry the effects of our fallenness into everything we do, we are still intended to be co-creators and to make right choices. The strongest factors determining the way we treat nature are often our understanding of God and of humanity. And this is not only true of those of us who have a religion. The majority in the West who claim no practical allegiance to any God still put an active faith in the belief that there is no higher being who in his wisdom has set down rules and laws which are good and wise in themselves. This leaves mankind to determine his own rules for living and relating to his surroundings which will be based on a variety of factors, and in a world dominated by the Post-modern, will be different for everyone. In such a world it seems necessary to have some kind of ethical system which is usually based upon the utilitarian ideal that the route to determining the right course of action is plotted by examining the consequences. The goal might be something like the classical maxim, 'the greatest good for the greatest number of people,' but in such a fluid system where racial and sexual factors often place the least value upon the weakest members of society or upon the environment which cannot speak for itself or possesses no intrinsic monetary value, the end result tends towards exploitation. What is more, since there is no means of assigning an absolute value to anything, the system contains a built-in inertia through lack of consensus, and is often a recipe for conflict, compromise and frustration. Thus, where there is no belief in a creator, and a resultant understanding that the creation has an inherent purpose to it, humanity feels free to impose its own purposes upon it and use it for its own purposes.

For those who claim a faith, the kind of God they believe in can have a tremendous (although often subconscious) impact upon the way they view the world. Belief in a high and transcendent God encourages his followers to adopt attitudes to the environment which are akin to traditional Greek philosophy. Either God does not mind how we adapt our environment because he is outside the machine and has no desire to be involved with it, or it does not matter to him because he is a spiritual entity who can have nothing to do with the material world. In this kind of thinking the spiritual life is all that is important, and salvation is often an entirely personal concept which has little bearing on the way we treat matter. We, in this system, are kings; and have few responsibilities toward non-human creation.

At the opposite end of the spectrum is the pantheist view in which all things are god, or at least part of him. Apart from the fact that this is unbiblical it is also reductionist since, in practice, to see all life as having an equivalent value in its essence tends to lead us along the road towards the extremist views of various pressure groups whose members might insist that the life of a monkey in a laboratory is of equivalent value to the life of the scientist who experiments on him. This is reductionist because it tends to lead the believer in the cause to condone the killing or injuring of the scientist on a like for like basis. Lynn White argues that animists had a due respect for nature before Christianity 'enlightened' them to believe otherwise, and he suggests that this was due to their pantheist beliefs. This is true, but even he recognizes that civilization has come too far down its present track to attempt a retreat to an alternative religion – especially the religion of the forest which is meaningless in the city. No, White implores Christians to reform their Christianity along less exploitative lines, and that is what I have sought to do by leaving behind the extremes of transcendence and pantheism and returning to the Old Testament records.

Without doubt we need to hold up our hands and confess that much of our Western Christianity has failed to appreciate and understand its heritage. This suggests that in environmental terms it has been more an ecological fool than a wise steward.[97] But history records that things have not been quite as bleak as White suggests. There have been worthy Western traditions which have stood out prophet-like in the wilderness. Two of the founding Fathers of the church provided a basis which might have been built on; when both Irenaeus[98] and Athenasius[99] taught that nature had a part in God's purposes. In more recent times the Quaker and Mennonite movements have been amongst those who taught the love of God for all creation, and the example of the Benedictines, Cistercians and Franciscans – the founder of which Lynn White champions as the 'patron saint of ecologists'[100] have been equally challenging. Unfortunately these voices were not incorporated into the mainstream but instead became the inspiration for 'a mind-

131

centred, and ultimately manipulative, *observation* of nature.'[101]

Despite the failings of the West, we are not left bereft of ideas, for

> Christendom has not been without a consistent, coherent, and ancient tradition of the involvement of humanity in the redemption of creation. That idea has been maintained as an important part of Eastern Orthodox theology.[102]

Because Eastern Orthodoxy has remained untainted by the West's infatuation with personal experience and individual salvation it provides us with a wellspring of new ideas. It has also been the inspiration behind many of the recent theological works I have referred to. From within the Eastern tradition come ideas which are strangely compelling. We find, for example, the belief that humans are like priests lifting nature to God in a cosmic sacrament of worship and praise. In this way the Eastern Orthodox Christian is sensitive to matter and its relationship with the creator and is concerned that all things should receive the touch of his blessing. Within this tradition humanity takes upon itself the role of mediator between God and nature, and recognizes that 'the mastery over nature must be held within the mystery of worship. Otherwise we lose both mastery and mystery.'[103]

Although Eastern Orthodoxy might have provided the inspiration for our rediscovery of these insights, much of the work we have referred to has been distinctly Western. Wilkinson is right when he states that:

> the church needs both Eastern and Western theology. We need the rich orthodox development of the biblical concept of the redemption of all creation through men and women, as they are redeemed through Christ. And we need the Western church's development of radical, but responsible, individuality – an individuality for purposes of sacrifice and service, for the tending of creation, not its domination.[104]

White himself suggests this when he states in his summary sentence 'The Greek saint contemplates; The Western saint acts.'[105] Although he goes on to use this observation as a stick to beat the Western saint who acted wrongly, the logical extension of this comment is that the West is well placed to play a part in saving the world from continued exploitation. As I have sought to contrive a new model out of the best insights contained within the wealth of more recent theological material from within my own tradition – but which themselves reach back into the Eastern Christian tradition – it has seemed to me that the best label to attach to the result is found in the stewardship motif. This is despite the fact that the stewardship idea has been dismissed by some for being simply a new nameplate on the old ideas of human domination.[106] This admittedly has the weakness of leaving *responsibility* in the hands of imperfect humanity, but in what other hands could it be left since it is men and women who have been entrusted with the task of stewardship? My hope is that it is the marriage of Eastern and Western traditions which will provide a correction to past misunderstandings and overemphases within both traditions. I also expect that with a new emphasis upon contemplation,[107] relationship, responsibility, accountability and covenant blessing; the stewardship idea will plough a unique and influential furrow. It is well placed to do this because at its heart is a set of absolute values which, although an unpopular concept today, means that the model is essentially practical in nature and therefore can be applied to each new issue as it emerges. The fact that a central characteristic of a steward is that he is responsible to another for the way he exercises his stewardship also means that failure to act correctly has moral consequences in addition to the legal and causal constraints which are the only restrictions available within a human centred value system.[108] The idea of human stewards seems to be the ideal combination of servant, manager, guardian and farmer of the diverse and valuable creation that longs for the sons of God to reveal godly principles of dominion.

Notes

1. Origen – *Contra Celsum*. IV. 75. trans. H. Chadwick. (Cambridge. 1953) p 243.
2. Augustine – *Soliloquies*. 1, xiv, 24. In Erich Przywara – *An Augustine Synthesis*. (Sheed and Ward. New York. 1945) p 1.
3. Francis Bacon – *Religious Meditations*. in Spedding, Ellis & Heath – *The Works of Francis Bacon*. Vol. 7. p 253.
4. Francis Bacon – *Novum Organum*. Aphorism. cxxix; Works. Vol. 4. p 114.
5. Passmore – *Man's Responsibility for Nature – Ecological Problems and Western Traditions* (Scribner. New York. 1974) p 27.
6. Ibid. pp 16-17.
7. See Sean McDonagh – *The Greening of the Church*. (Geoffrey Chapman. London. 1990) p 121.
8. Gerhard von Rad – *Genesis*. (SCM. London. 1972). p 59.
9. Genesis 1:26.
10. Claus Westermann – *Genesis 1-11*. (SPCK. London. 1984) p 158.
11. Psalm 8:6.
12. Wilkinson. *Earthkeeping in the Nineties* (Eerdmans, Grand Rapids, Michegan 1992) p 287.
13. Von Rad. op. cit. (1972) p 60; Westermann op. cit. (1984) p 161.
14. Lawrence Osborn – *Meeting God in Creation*. (Grove. Nottingham. 1990) p 9.
15. James Barr – 'Man and Nature – The Ecological Controversy and the Old Testament.' *Bulletin of the John Rylands University Library of Manchester*. Vol. 55. Autumn 1972. No. 1. p 22. See also Westermann op. cit. (1984) pp 158, 9.
16. William Dyrness – 'Stewardship of the Earth in the Old Testament.' in Wesley Granberg-Michaelson (ed.) – *Tending the Garden. Essays on the Gospel and the Earth*. op. cit. p 53. See also Deuteronomy 17:14-20; Psalm 72:1-3, 16.
17. Dyrness. op. cit. (1987) p 53.
18. Philippians 2:6-8.
19. See, for example, Welbourn op. cit. pp 564-5.
20. Anne Primavesi – 'Attending and Tending.' *The Way*. Vol 31. October 1991. No 4. p 295.
21. Numbers 32:22, 29; I Chronicles 22:18; Joshua 18:1.
22. 2 Chronicles 28:10; Nehemiah 5:5; Jeremiah 34:11, 16.
23. Esther 7:8.
24. Micah 7:10; 2 Samuel 8:11; Zechariah 9:15.
25. Barr. op. cit. (1972) p 22.
26. Dyrness. op. cit. (1987) p 54.
27. e.g. Ezekiel 34.

28. Steve Bishop – 'Green Theology and Deep Ecology: New Age or New Creation?' *Themelios*. April/May 1991. Vol 16. No 3. p 9.
29. Genesis 1:29, 30.
30. Westermann. op. cit. (1984) p 54.
31. Genesis 2:19.
32. Christopher Wright – *Living as the People of God. The Relevance of Old Testament Ethics*. (IVP. Leicester. 1983) p 70.
33. Matthew 25:14-30.
34. Francis Schaeffer – *Pollution and the Death of Man*. (Tyndale. Wheaton, Illinois. 1970) p 69-70.
35. H. Paul Santmire – 'Healing The Protestant Mind. Beyond the Theology of Human Dominion.' in ed. Hessel. *After Nature's Revolt. Eco-Justice and Theology*. (Fortress Press. Mineapolis, Minnesota. 1992) p 75.
36. Ibid. p 76.
37. Douglas John Hall – *Imaging God*. (Friendship Press. New York. 1996) p 112.
38. Colin Brown. (ed.) – *New International Dictionary of New Testament Theology*. Vol. 1. (Zondervan. Grand Rapids, Michigan. 1986) p 365.
39. 1 Samuel 18:3; 20:8.
40. Genesis 21:22-24; 26:26ff; 1 Kings 5:12; 20:34.
41. 2 Kings 11:4; 1 Samuel 11:1; 2 Samuel 3:12f.
42. e.g. Exodus 19:3-9, 24:3-8. etc.
43. Genesis 6:18.
44. 2 Kings 13:23.
45. Jeremiah 33:21.
46. e.g. Jeremiah 50:5.
47. e.g. Jeremiah 11:4; 24:7; 30:22; Ezekiel 11:20; 14:11; Zechariah 8:8. etc.
48. 2 Kings 23:1-3.
49. Genesis 6:18.
50. Genesis 9:1-17.
51. Dumbrell – *Covenant and Creation. An Old Testament Covenantal Theology* (Paternoster. Exeter. 1984) p 32.
52. McDonagh. op. cit. (1990) p 124.
53. Dumbrell. op. cit. (1984) p 43, 27.
54. George Kehm – 'The New Story. Redemption as Fulfilment of Creation.' in Hessel. op. cit. p 93.
55. Von Rad. op. cit. (1972) p 130.
56. Genesis 15 and 17.
57. Exodus 19:5.
58. Park – *Caring for Creation* (Marshals. London. 1992) p 135.
59. See for example Leviticus 25:23 and the Parable of the Tenants in Matthew 21:33ff.
60. Deuteronomy 11:12.
61. Genesis 1:22, 24, 28.

62. See Galatians 3-4.
63. Leviticus 25:23.
64. Park. op. cit. (1992) pp 138-140.
65. Leviticus 22:27-28.
66. Deuteronomy 22:6-7.
67. Deuteronomy 22:10.
68. Deuteronomy 25:4.
69. Proverbs 12:10.
70. Isaiah 28:26.
71. Exodus 23:10, 11.
72. Leviticus 25:4-7.
73. Leviticus 25:18-22.
74. Leviticus 26:32-35.
75. Exodus 23:12.
76. Wilkinson. op. cit. (1992) p 26-32.
77. David Pimental et al – 'Land Degradation. Effects on Food and Energy Resources.' *Science*. 194. (1976) pp 149-155.
78. Walther Zimmerli – 'The Place and Limit of the Wisdom in the Framework of the Old Testament Theology.' in *Scottish Journal of Theology*. No 17. (1964) p 148.
79. Gerhard von Rad – *Wisdom in Israel*. [trans. James Martin] (Abingdon Press. Nashville, Tennesee. 1972) p 7.
80. Proverbs 8:1-6, 22, 23, 30, 31, 33.
81. 1 Kings 4:32, 33.
82. Gerhard von Rad – 'Job XXXVIII and Ancient Egyptian Wisdom.' in *The Problem of the Hextateuch and Other Essays*. (Oliver & Boyd. London. 1965) p 287.
83. 1 Kings 10.
84. Robert Johnston – in Granberg-Michaelson (ed.) – *Tending the Garden*. (Eerdmans. Grand Rapids, Michigan. 1987) p 70.
85. Job 38-41.
86. Job 38:26.
87. John Austin Baker – 'Biblical views of Nature.' in – *Liberating Life*. Birch, Eakin & McDaniel (Orbis. Maryknoll, New York. 1990) p 17.
88. Walter B. Gulick – 'The Bible and Ecological Spirituality.' *Theology Today*. July 1991. p 189.
89. Ibid. p 190.
90. Job 38:33; 41:9.
91. Amos 4:6-9. Susan Gillingham – 'Who makes the morning darkness: God and Creation in the book of Amos.' *Scottish Journal of Theology*. Vol 45. No 2. 1992. (T&T Clark. Edinburgh. 1992) p 168.
92. Ibid. p 183.
93. Romans 8.

God's Covenant with Creation

94. Jürgen Moltmann – *The Crucified God. The Cross as the Foundation and Criticism of Christian Theology.* (SCM Press. London. 1974) p 222.
95. Gregorios. *The Human Presence.* (WCC. Geneva. 1978) p 70.
96. Dyrness. op. cit. (1987) p 57.
97. James Crampsey suggests that the Parable of the Rich Fool (Luke 12:16-20) is God's rebuke on the rich man's exercise of dominion. This strong denunciation (Matthew 5:21-22) comes to any man who treats creation with the attitude, 'What's in it for me?' See James Crampsey – 'Look at the Birds of the air. . .' *The Way.* Vol. 31. October 1991. No. 4. p 287.
98. Edward Rocie Hardy (ed.) – *Against Hereses. Early Christian Fathers.* – vol. 1. (Westminster Press. Philadelphia, Pennsylvania. 1955). p 385. and Irenaeus – *Against Hereses.* V.xviii.3.
99. Athenasius – *On the Incarnation.* p 26.
100. Lynn White Jr. – The Historical Roots of our Ecological Crisis. *Science.* 10 March 1967. vol.155. No 3767. p 1207.
101. Wilkinson. op. cit. (1992) p 302.
102. Ibid. p 303.
103. Gregorios. op. cit. (1978) p 89.
104. Wilkinson. op. cit. (1992) p 306.
105. White. op. cit. p 1206.
106. Most notable amongst the critics of a continuing fascination with the stewardship ideal is H. Paul Santmire, who (in *The Travail of Nature* and other essays and articles) states his belief that the idea of stewardship fails to deliver the goods because it is itself based on the theme of human dominion – which he rejects because of the fact that despite the best efforts of many theologians it seems impossible to extricate the doctrine from the idea of domination. This, he believes, is because the doctrine simply limits behaviour, therefore implying that nature still has only instrumental value. (See for example *The Travail of Nature.* op. cit. p 182-3; and the article 'Healing the Protestant Mind.' in Hessel – *After Nature's Revolt. Eco-Justice and Theology.* op. cit. p 60, 61-63.) Whilst I sympathize with Santmire, I do not think this fact alone justifies the ditching of the stewardship motif.
107. I agree with Santmire that our understanding of stewardship needs to encompass the theme of contemplation in order to make it less utilitarian. (Hessel. op. cit. p 60-65.) But I do not agree that my attempts to qualify the meaning of dominion show the weaknesses of the theology itself. This is because what I am attempting to do is rediscover what I believe to be an original intention of the biblical writer, not invent a new meaning in the light of the current environmental problems.
108. See Sam Berry – 'Environmental knowledge, attitudes and action: A code of practice' *Scientific Public Affairs.* 5(2) 13-23 1990. p 17.

CHAPTER FOUR

~

The Promise of Redemption

The Hope of Redemption

*'Sins' are in truth only the symptoms, the passing rash that
lets us know that the schizophrenia, the angst still goes on.
'Sins' are not to be dwelt on, but cleared up as soon as possible,
so that mankind can get on with finding the way through the
distortion of good to achieve what is good in itself.[1]*

So far we have looked at what the universe was created to be,
what went wrong with that ideal and the means God used
to limit the effects of sin. But this is not the end of the story.
We have already noted the possibility that Genesis 3 points
forward and contains the seeds of creation's hope of salvation
with what may be a messianic pre-echo in Genesis 3:15.[2]
However, the immediate story resumes with the expulsion of
fallen humanity from the garden. But the passage also contains
signs that God is prepared to adapt himself to the new state of
affairs between himself and mankind, since God responds to
Adam's sin by providing clothes to cover the shame felt by
Adam and Eve at their nakedness.[3] Then in Chapter 4 God
intervenes again, and protects Cain from unjust retribution –
even though his fear was brought upon himself by his own
disobedience.[4] As Genesis unfolds we see the outlining of the
first of God's post-Fall covenants with humanity in chapter 9;
and later in the Old Testament emerges a system of laws and
principles which, as we have already seen, are intended to
provide the basis for mankind's just and righteous behaviour
towards the whole of creation. Finally we note the emergence
of political systems aimed at policing these laws and providing
a structure that ensures accountability. But this is all aimed at
placing limits on the effects of sin.

141

It is not until we turn to the New Testament that we find the sprouting of these seeds of creation's future hope, and note that this hope is ultimately founded upon the work of God in Christ, as he reconciles the world to himself. So whilst it is true that mankind has responsibilities for creation, its future is not solely and ultimately determined by human activity. All creation – human, and non-human, animate and inanimate – looks to God for its final destiny.

Returning to Romans 8, verses 18 and 19 we read: 'I consider that our present sufferings are not worth comparing with the glory that will be revealed in us. The creation waits in eager expectation for the sons of God to be revealed.' First we see mention of the hope of redemption – and note Paul's deliberate reference to 'the whole created universe and not just, indeed not specially, the human part of it.'[5] The fact that creation's hope (verse 20) is placed alongside human hope (verse 23) is significant, and surely indicates that the redemption which the non-human creation anticipates is at least as real, and on a par with, the hope that is in the hearts of God's people. This is not at all surprising, for if God still delights in his creation, as we suggested in the first part of this study, it is only reasonable to suppose that he is offended when it is destroyed, and calls his own people to free it from oppression.[6] But, if we are to serve creation as God wishes, the maxim that God is served in and through the service we offer to our neighbour[7] will need to be understood in a new way. Specifically, the distinction we often make between caring for human beings and caring for creation will need erasing in the recognition that God calls us to do both. As John Cobb says: 'when we make possible the healthy functioning of the biosphere, God enjoys the vitality.'[8]

But how does verse 19 tell us this redemption is to be brought about? The clear answer from the text is that the 'sons of God' are to produce this freedom, which evidently refers to those whom God has adopted as his sons and daughters –

God's redeemed community.[9] And when will this happen? When does this 'revealing' take place? The common view is that the writer is looking ahead to the time when God will reveal his redeemed people to the unredeemed – at the time of the final judgement. But if we take Jesus' teaching on the Kingdom of God seriously, Jesus' second coming will not be the arrival of the Kingdom, but the completion of the Kingdom of God which has already begun.[10] So this present age is one which is characterized by Kingdom blessings.[11] Whether this view of the 'now, and yet still to come' Kingdom takes the form of C.H. Dodd's 'realized eschatology' or R.H. Fuller's 'inaugurated eschatology' is unimportant. What is important is that both Acts and the Pauline epistles are founded upon the belief that the Kingdom of God is very much something that is already present in power, and is therefore a 'present reality of redemption.'[12]

Albert Wolters contrasts his view of the Kingdom of God with four other 'restricted views' which are also current in modern thinking.[13] The first he labels the 'pietist' view which is based upon the Authorized Bible's rendering of Luke 17:21. 'Behold the kingdom of God is *within* you (author's italics).' This is restricted because the sphere of the activity of the kingdom is limited to the inner life of the soul alone. The second, taught by Roman Catholicism (although modified by Vatican II) – but followed by others as well – identifies the kingdom with the institutionalized church. Thus only that work which is pursued directly on behalf of the church is thought to be part of God's kingdom. The third restrictive view is the dispensationalist tendency to restrict the kingdom to the future millennium – which has the practical effect of limiting the value and scope of human intervention in the present. The final alternative is held by classical liberal protestants and liberation theologians who attach 'the name 'Kingdom of God' to anything that seems humane and progressive from a humanistic point of view.'[14] This postmillennial ideal removes any eschatological hope of divine intervention, and places its expectations wholly on mankind to heal our environment.

I am convinced that Wolters is right when he insists that his understanding of the Kingdom of God is an important key to the adoption of an ecologically caring theology. The problem is that what Wolters calls 'two-realm theories' restrict the scope of Christ's Lordship. 'Again and again Christians find ways of excluding certain areas or dimensions of their lives and the life of their culture from the need for reform for Christ's sake.'[15] It is essential that we remove all Greek forms of division in our thinking. The Kingdom of God is here now, and encompasses all things – not just soul, church, the future or political revolution. It is also essential that we recognize that the eschatology promoted by these 'two-realm' theories is not as material as that found in the New Testament. As Patrick Nullens insists:

> Through the incarnation of Christ, creation was reaffirmed, and through his resurrection, the foundation has been laid for a material eschatology.[16]

I believe that as we see the Kingdom of God in these terms it will also be impossible to read Jesus' insistence that the Kingdom of God has arrived[17] and, at the same time, to believe that the revealing of the sons of God is an event which is entirely in the future. It is true that Paul must be looking forward to a time when creation will finally and fully be restored (at the second coming of Christ) but since the sons of God are those who are led by his Spirit;[18] he must also mean that God's redeemed humanity is called and empowered to act responsibly towards creation in this present age as a sign of the age to come. And one of the things the Spirit leads them to do must surely be to enact the Old Testament principles of correct stewardship. It is only then that the sons of God will be shown to be what they are – followers of the precepts of God and those who 'for those with eyes to see . . . constitute a sign of hope.'[19]

The promise of Redemption touches creation in two ways. The first is through its effect upon us. When God is allowed to touch a human life, and it becomes submitted to him through faith in Christ and indwelt with the Holy Spirit, a process of salvation begins. Whilst the main focus of this process is the final hope of the salvation that is still to come, it also has a renewing effect in the present. This is how the 'sons of God' are enabled to rise above their fallen urges and respond to God's call to care for nature. The second way nature is touched is by the direct intervention of God and, according to the eschatology of both Peter and John, the hope of redemption currently anticipated by the whole creation will only be fully met when Christ returns.[20]

The Christian faith is all about the present and future history of Redemption, experienced in embryonic form in the present, but yet to be completed in the future. Thus it is a religion based on divine promises. This is important, and nowhere do we find this theme more clearly and vividly expressed than in the writings of Jürgen Moltmann. In *Theology of Hope*[21] we find a work in which history and eschatology are bound together into a compelling synthesis. In making this bond Moltmann is able to break free from the shackles of the kind of hope for the future which preoccupies itself with simply making the present bearable whilst we wait for God to intervene at some point in the future. The hope Moltmann writes about is a more immediate entity because he prefers to focus our eyes on a more compelling horizon – reminding us that Christianity is a religion that 'announces the coming of a reality that does not yet exist'[22] whilst reminding us that in Christ, God has identified himself with his suffering world and now in his Trinitarian being 'his love embraces the world in all its negativity, suffers the contradiction and overcomes it.'[23]

So Moltmann's response to evil in the world is to assert that 'the cross means that instead of overcoming evil by suppressing evildoers, God overcomes evil by embracing evildoers in his love and bearing the pain . . . God is this suffering love.'[24] This means that it is only as the Christian focuses his eyes on this future horizon that he becomes bound to the future and develops a sense for an eschatological history which is linear and not cyclical. This gives birth to a faith that this future will be better than the present and, despite appearances to the contrary, is sure and certain because it is bound up with the promises of an omniscient and omnipotent God.

The basis for Moltmann's certainty is found in his understanding of the resurrection of the crucified Christ. He is deeply critical of the modern historical approach to the resurrection[25] and of the Existentialist approach to its existential significance. That God *seems* to be dead both in history and in our experience is understandable, but it is so 'only in the world as the cross shows it to be.'[26] If we remain locked into our present experience of the world, there is no basis for any true hope. But since the cross is not the end of the story in the Gospel accounts, neither is it the end of hope. for death gives way to resurrection. It is the resurrection of Jesus that 'is the beginning and source of the abolition of the Universal Good Friday.'[27] So 'the world in which God is apparent, the world which corresponds to God and proves God, is not the world as it is, but the *new creation* promised in Jesus' resurrection.'[28]

So on the cross Jesus identified with our lack of hope. Then three days later God transfigured this reality by raising him from the tomb. And it is this dialectic of cross and resurrection which opens the way for any hope of an ecologically just future. For, the resurrection promises a hope which depends on a truly transcendent God for its fulfilment,[29] and also opens the door for human engagement in bringing that future into being.

Creation's hope emerges out of the tension between present

reality and a faith in the vision of a just future that is promised by the God who follows the cross with the resurrection. And this eschatological spirit[30] reveals the future to be both open and provisional, which in turn gives the Christian the motivation to suffer both the inherent contradiction between the now and not yet, and the persecution delivered to all eschatological visionaries who must necessarily live both in conflict with the world as it is and as prophets at the vanguard of change.[31]

This tension between the present and the future reveals an eschatological dilemma. Who is it that produces the change we hope for – ourselves or God? The view we take on this question rather depends on our preferred interpretation of the 'Kingdom of God' metaphor. If we prefer the Premillennial equating of the Kingdom as something brought in by God at some point in the future, the scope for human co-operation will be minimal. Whereas if we choose the other, Postmillennial, extreme, all hope is placed upon us as our own saviours since we are responsible for ushering in the state of 'heaven on earth' as we tread the path of progressive enlightenment. As I stated earlier, the view of the Kingdom of God I prefer brings redemption into the present and therefore 'understands the promise as a divine initiative which creates a human initiative for real historical change.'[32]

This produces a view of the world that 'is full of real, but not yet actual possibilities, that is, possibilities whose conditions have not yet fully emerged'[33] but which surface when we co-operate with God. In his later works Moltmann indicates his belief that it is the Church which, together with Christ, is the mediator that brings the eschatological future into the present.[34] But the future emerges both out of tendencies seen in the present[35] and from (presently) unrevealed potentialities.[36] And the only thing that gives rise to this sort of future is hope, because mere human planning without the eschatological vision hope brings can only succeed in perpetuating the status quo. Only hope can produce the kind of anticipation that is able to unite present action with future intervention in a way which is vast enough to promise the transformation of the whole cosmos.

And it is this tension which Lynn White's 'Western saint'[37] finds so hard to live with. Human reaction to crisis – whether ecological or otherwise – is to do something, blame someone, act or react. In his later book which he subtitles *An Ecological Doctrine of Creation*,[38] Moltmann isolates, not God's six days of activity, but his one day of rest as being the true foundation of salvation; and shows how it is rest and contemplation that opens creation to its eschatological future. 'On the sabbath the redemption of the world is celebrated in anticipation. The sabbath is itself the presence of eternity in time, and a foretaste of the world to come.'[39] Moltmann calls the sabbath the 'feast of creation'. meaning that it is both a celebration of completion and a promise of a redemption that is still to come.

At the end of the sixth day Moltmann contests that the creation was still incomplete – despite the fact that it was perfectly formed. Its completion came when God took a rest from his creating and stood aside from his work in order to *experience* or *feel* his creation. As he does so, God 'adopts the community of creation as his own milieu. In his rest he is close to the movement of them all.'[40] Perhaps this is the point at which the relationship between God and creation begins to develop – in much the same way as a new-born studies its mother's face as it sucks her breast, and as it does so recalls her (previously disembodied) voice.[41] Whatever image we choose, 'creation can be seen as God's revelation of his works; but it is only the sabbath that is God's revelation of God's self. That is why the works of creation flow into the sabbath of creation.'[42]

It is from this rest and the unfolding relationship between

creator and creation that God's blessing is mediated. And this blessing is not given directly to us, which might imply that God blesses so that in return we can do something for God; but it is placed on a day, the sabbath. This first of all makes the blessing universal – for all creation; and also means that it is a blessing placed upon our whole existence, as long as it is in resting, not activity, that we find our sustaining foundation and the centre of our being.

This is precisely the point at which Western society is weakest. We prefer to reward work and achievement and keep rest as a regrettable interruption to our productivity because rest is thought of as non-productive and (ironically) uncreative. But the feast of the sabbath shows rest to be creative because it is only as we pause to watch and reflect that we are able to seek and discover a restored relationship with God, and are therefore able to appreciate the true meaning and value of creation. It is here that the anticipation of a future hope is burned into our souls.

And it is here too that we gain a true perspective of God's work of redeeming fallen creation. When we read that God made the seventh day holy[43] Moltmann concludes that the writer means that God made the day his special property. It is this interpretation of the day that is reflected throughout the Old Testament. God first applies the sabbath to humanity in the fourth, and longest, of the Ten Commandments,[44] and its place at the centre of the law implies that:

> it is impossible to celebrate and enjoy it at the cost of other people. The feast can only be celebrated and enjoyed together with all the others. If human beings are to 'have dominion' over the animals, here animals are to enjoy the sabbath too.[45]

This weekly sabbath, which Moltmann calls 'the Jewish doctrine of justification by God's grace'[46] later points the way to the sabbath year[47] in which the land is allowed to celebrate its freedom; and the year of jubilee[48] in which liberty was restored to all people and land.

So this feast of the sabbath can be seen as the symbol of inner liberty from the human obsession to justify our own existence by continually competing and producing. And it also points forward to the promise of God's future redemption of all things from the slavery of sin. In recognition of this Moltmann refers to redemption as 'the eternal sabbath'[49] – the time when creation and revelation are one. The reason I have spent so long on the hope of redemption before exploring the theme of redemption itself is because this is precisely the point at which we currently find ourselves. We await, in the words of Paul, 'a glory that will be revealed.'[50] And however certain that hope is, 'it remains a hope, not a present possession.'[51] But the sabbath does not just point to the past and the future. It also 'opens that creation for the coming Kingdom of God.'[52] We will now consider how salvation is to be brought to God's creation.

Repentance

Humanity needs redeeming because we have lost our relationship with God and cannot regain it ourselves. The realm of nature needs redeeming because it too has been cut off from its creator and also experiences the tyranny of its oppressors. But whilst the whole of creation awaits its final liberation, God's grace is being poured out upon the earth as people return to him in a spirit of repentance. Where there is repentance, it implies that something has taken place in the human spirit which recognizes the presence and effect of sin. For example in Acts 2, when Peter was explaining the events of Pentecost to the assembled crowd he catalogues their disobedience – and as he does so the people are convicted of their error. Repentance is a natural step once this revelation has occurred.

We have a great deal to repent of. We are guilty of

cosmological dualism[53] 'which was as alien to ancient Israel as it should become to us,'[54] and of a human centredness and individualism which has often reduced the gospel to a message of human and individual salvation and which has failed to see that God's intention is wider and deeper than our short-term happiness. Our theology has also tended towards fatalism on one hand – especially where extreme Calvinist or Dispensationalist[55] tendencies have encouraged us to believe that it does not matter what we do to the earth; and undue romanticism on the other – which fails to acknowledge our sinful heritage and its distorting effects. We are also guilty of distorting particular doctrines for our own ends. Critics are right to point to the fact that theology has been used to justify our domination of the earth – confusing it with the injunction that we are to have dominion over it. Thus we have become permanent squatters upon the earth over which we were put as tenants. In short, we have neglected our theological heritage and kicked over the traces.

Without repentance there can be no real change, because without it there is no admission of error and no indwelling power to live differently. Repentance is most frequently encouraged in the New Testament by use of the Greek word *metanoia* – meaning 'to turn around.' George Tinker argues that the underlying sense of this word is best given by the Aramaic word *shuv* (meaning 'to return') thus adding to the Greek notion of 'change of mind.'[56] So true repentance involves action: specifically a return to God and a new determination to live within the boundaries which we have previously transgressed. It therefore means a commitment to live justly and responsibly.[57]

So in practical terms, this returning to a biblical world view includes erasing the line we find it so easy to draw between concern for human life and a concern for other living creatures, when we should be concerned for both together. It also means seeing ourselves as 'communal beings constituted by our relations with others,'[58] and living by a received wisdom which informs us about what is good and right and puts limits on our behaviour. Repentance will also lead us to commit ourselves to building a new theology which is based upon principles uncovered from the old but related specifically to the modern world. We will then be clearing the way for the indwelling Spirit of God to produce the kind of identification with the afflictions of the poor and downtrodden (in the whole of creation) which characterized the ministry of Jesus and fulfils our intended ministry of reconciling the whole earth to Christ.[59]

But how does such a change come about? How can we suddenly change the actions of many centuries? All change begins with a revised attitude which comes about as we see things differently. And the most personal revision mankind has to make is in the way we view ourselves – and that is where we must begin.

Redeeming Mankind

The term 'redemption' is a particularly apposite one because of its overtones of buying back, or returning to a state of rightness. It has been my concern throughout this study to uncover biblical ideas about God and his creation in order that we might recover an appreciation of what God is doing in the work of redemption. It would have been easy to do as some have done, and simply add a concern for creation to our already cluttered agenda – as if it were a peripheral issue meriting the special attention of only a few fanatics. But mankind, Christians included, do not so much need to be reintroduced to nature as reconciled with it. And before that is possible a revision of thinking is needed in our understanding of how redemption touches us and the moulds the way we view our world.

When we looked at what it means to be human, the image of God motif played a central part. If we recall the discoveries we made and their importance to our self-understanding, it is perhaps no great surprise to find that the image of God metaphor reappears in the New Testament to describe God's intention for redeemed humanity. So in Colossians 3 Paul implores his readers not to defile themselves or abuse others 'since you have taken off your old self with its practices, and have put on the new self, which is being renewed in knowledge in the image of its creator.'[60] The key to correct behaviour here is the recognition that the image of God in us and others is precious and needs affirming and renewing, not denying or debasing.

It is the coming of Jesus that takes the image one step further. The New Testament gives many titles to Jesus. One of them is the name 'Second Adam'[61] and another is the 'image of God.'[62] The title 'Second Adam' refers to the fact that Christ's solidarity with humanity is of the same order as Adam's:

> For if by the trespass of the one man, death reigned through that one man, how much more will those who receive God's abundant provision of grace and of the gift of righteousness reign in life through the one man, Jesus Christ.[63]

But, on the other hand, when Paul describes Jesus as 'the image of the invisible God' he is clearly meaning that Christ is a perfect representation of the Father in a way that the Genesis writer was not implying when he describes humanity as being created 'in God's image'. Thus since, by virtue of his very nature, Christ is perfectly equipped to be a mediator between God and his creation; he is uniquely able to pick up both ends of what we might visualize as being a severed thread and effect a restoration of all that was lost by Adam. It is this perfect image of God who now takes on the mantle Adam threw off.

As the image of the invisible God, Christ is the mediator in creation, the reconciler of the world, the Lord of the divine rule. God appears in his perfect image, God rules through this image, God reconciles and redeems through his image on the earth.[64]

What is more, the image of God title given to Jesus makes the image of God motif easier to picture because we know a great deal more about Jesus than we do about an ideal humanity in the original creation purposes of God. And since Christ is the perfect image of God, it is now no surprise to discover that the new human calling is to become the image of Christ[65] 'and through this enter upon the path which will make us *gloria Dei* on earth.'[66] In Romans 8 the *gloria Dei* consists in behaving in a Christ-like way as we are led and empowered by the Holy Spirit. In practical terms this calling parallels the cultural mandate we read about in Genesis 1 to rule the earth whilst recognizing Christ's lordship over all things.[67] But before it becomes possible to exercise correct stewardship it is also necessary for us to revise the way we view the world beyond ourselves.

Ronald Manahan indicates how the ancient Near East web of accountability helps us to see the way our complex spectrum of relationships both breaks down and is remade.[68] In the system he outlines, there were always those to whom each individual owed obedience, and others towards whom beneficence was expected. Where the required obedience is present, the result is that blessing is meted out to the individual and, by extension, to the one whom he was expected to bless. But where there is a disruption of this network by wilful disobedience, the web of caring is harmed and the flow of blessing is interrupted.[69] The web is only restored when the individual at the centre recovers his understanding of what is required.

If we give identities to each group (God as the one who must be obeyed, and the poor, the disadvantaged and the powerless as the ones who must be served) it becomes easy to see how an individual's sin affects others who may be entirely innocent. It is also salutary to reflect upon the observation that where we have seen the rise of the idols of freedom, individualism and rampant materialism, there has often been a corresponding lack of concern for this 'lower' stratum. But redemption, beginning as it does with the renewal of the mind and its attitudes[70] and rooted as it is in fulfilling God's requirements laid down at the beginning of creation,[71] opens the way for responsible behaviour towards all things.

So we really have come full circle – except that the idea of stewardship is no longer an ideal which has been lost in the mists of time, but is now a goal made possible when Christ redeems fallen humanity. But there are still great problems – not all things have been redeemed (nor will they be until the Lord of Creation brings all things under his control); and the image of God in redeemed humanity, although on the mend, is not complete. So before I move on to the redemption of nature I want to focus on two themes which might help in this healing and are part and parcel of the renewal of our minds.

Loving Nature

In her article Loving Nature[72] Susan Bratton tackles the question of whether God loves his creation, and if so whether his love for human and non-human creation is the same. This she sees as the most important ethical question since love is the only proper motivation for Christian ethical behaviour, and is the true source of right relationships. In her evaluation of the writings of other theologians Bratton concludes that they usually take one of two paths. Some choose to suggest 'eros'[73] as the natural way for us to appreciate nature, since it incorporates the emotions (with which we experience nature) and, in keeping with Romans 1:20 'becomes a platform for understanding or reaching toward God.'[74]

But other theologians prefer to assume that we are called to love creation with an 'agape'[75] love – without going on to describe how *agape* can become a human response in a fallen world. As she examines the biblical records Bratton concludes that Christian love for nature should mirror that of the creator who, she indicates, loves his creation with *agape* love. *Eros*, she contends, is self-seeking and possessive and is therefore not a true embodiment of the Christ-like characteristics we are called to model. *Agape*, on the other hand, does not require reciprocity, equal status or common goals.

But since *eros* is a human love it expresses our natural fallen characteristics. And although *agape* love is a divine love, it always remains out of our reach – because by its very nature its expression is restricted to God. Bratton recognizes this, and instead of wishing things could be ideal, she argues that it is possible for us to love our fellow created beings with a combination of the two. *Eros* includes love of beauty, and as such is a proper part of our love for God and nature. But it is essential that we learn something of *agape* love because 'to pursue *eros* with nature, without pursuing *agape*, will eventually result in self-centred striving and ultimately damage the portion of creation one desires to love.'[76]

The *agape* dimension to love comes, not surprisingly, from God; and is given to us when in a spirit of repentant humility we take back upon ourselves the yoke of responsible stewardship, and rule the earth in the manner of a servant king.[77] So this agape love is more than an affection for, or a romanticizing of, nature; but is the key to the recovery of the long neglected way of giving practical expression to our new understanding of nature's value.

Valuing Nature

I have already shown how I believe the Fall damaged five key relationships, and in chapter 2, I examined Genesis 3 verse by verse, highlighting the implications of human disobedience. My main intention then was to examine the loss of relationship between God, humanity and the created order. But Ecofeminists take things one step further when they write about their belief that a domineering kind of dominion might also have its roots in the sexual conflict brought about by the Fall. They argue that it is the way we view creation that is unbalanced, and we *view* it wrongly because a male-dominated society naturally sees things from a predominantly male perspective. Anne Primavesi says that Ecofeminists

> assume that a balanced view of the world will integrate the contribution of women and the non-human world into human history, even where until now it has been largely ignored or devalued. Specifically, for example, Ecofeminists refuse to take the male relationship with creation as normative for the whole of humanity. Instead, they emphasize the essential and neglected role of women and nature within the human world view.[78]

So, Ecofeminism challenges us to ask whether Christianity is not a religion which is unduly dominated by pictures of masculine relationships with God. To argue their case, feminist theologians focus on the fact that Jesus was male and upon their belief that Christianity is ordered around 'men's exclusive possession of the Spirit handed on to them by the Son.'[79] The result of this overemphasis upon masculinity is then thought to be seen in a society that has become aggressively patriarchal because the (more) masculine traits of conquest, possession and an urge for power have predominated and even been encouraged and rewarded by successive cultures.[80]

Primavesi believes that the identity of the female then became linked with the private and domestic areas of life whilst the male identity became tied up with the (socially more important) public functions. Thus woman became classified as the 'weaker' sex in all respects. Woman also became identified with nature[81] – presumably by virtue of her shared fruitfulness and (enforced) passivity. The effect of this was to demean both female humanity and nature by labelling them weak, corrupt and secular. What is more, since the male was the more powerful and the self-appointed ruler, it was also assumed that the male relationship with both women and creation was normative.

I have no argument with the Ecofeminist's observation that society (and theology) is dominated by male images, and that this represents a grave error in our cultural and religious history. Where I am in disagreement however is that I believe that writers like Primavesi, Grey and Halkes have made a mistake when they begin with a valid observation, but then go on to try and prove that the problem was caused by the very enemy they have decided beforehand will be the culprit. So, to expose unduly masculine theology is to do Christian theology a service; but to blame a whole range of ecological ills on a 'Christocentricity [which] isolates the Trinity from the totality of divine relationship with the world,'[82] a God who is male and an incomplete canon [through sexist bias on the part of the compilers of scripture][83] is surely going too far. I also do not accept the idea that some of the features of society Primavesi classifies as uniquely male errors[84] would not have come about in a female-dominated society. Such developments in our culture have nothing to do with masculinity, but instead bear the marks of creatively independent humanity.

Humanity is fallen. Fallenness distorts humanity and our view of ourselves. Surely a truly Christian theology should be looking to discover the way the Fall has twisted our self-perception into oppressive forms which have resulted in both women and nature being demeaned and devalued. And the fact that we are now separated from the source of our human identity has also made theology an imperfect art; so that what the creator meant to reveal about himself has become deformed and fragmented – with some parts being misinterpreted and others overemphasized at the expense of less palatable themes.

So when God is (quite correctly) represented as Father, we now assume that God's intention was to imply that he exercises his fatherhood in a male way – as humans are used to picturing it – and that this means that God has masculine characteristics. Is it not a corruption of the human identity that we have converted the terms 'male' and 'female' into descriptions of opposing genders, given them both mutually exclusive characteristics and then labelled the male as representing the nature of God and therefore the most important of the two? We have already seen that it is sin that places distance between each individual and everything around him. Such distance leads to lack of understanding and appreciation, which in turn leads either to opposition, devaluation of the other or the desire to dominate and overpower.

But although I argue with some of the Ecofeminists' reasoning and with where they apportion the blame, I am convinced their thesis is important. Anne Primavesi does us a great service when she presents us with an alternative to the current state of affairs. She demands first of all 'that we refuse to fragment the world into isolated systems by separating ourselves from inert matter and other living organisms in a way which distances them from us.'[85]

The re-assignation of an intrinsic value to all things is an important part of the process of redemption since whole classes of creation have been marginalized as we have classified them as profane.

> The accepted reason for the 'profanity' of nature was that it became corrupted through Adam's sin. But whereas humanity was redeemed through baptism into Christ the Second Adam, nature remained unredeemed.[86]

If it is true that it is an overemphasis upon the masculine

that has made us think of nature as something with no rights of its own, and that this has brought about nature's despoliation; it might also be helpful for us to recall the fact that Eve was put into the garden by God to be Adam's helper. This presumably suggests that before Eve's creation Adam lacked something that her arrival put right. To this extent Adam and Eve were intended to be complementary partners. Perhaps this further indicates that when the Fall brought an enmity between the sexes Adam again became incomplete as long as he saw himself as Eve's master or competitor. So I conclude that in both human society and Christian Theology our aim should be to achieve a balanced synthesis between valuing and preserving nature on the one hand, and using it justly whilst ensuring its continued wholeness on the other.

Redeeming Nature

Redemption is all about removing the root of the problem and restoring a lost relationship with God. It is only then that it becomes possible to revise our wrong attitudes to the world in which we have been placed. But Christians are by no means in agreement that redemption is the best picture to use when talking about nature. There are many commentators, mainly of a dispensational persuasion, who believe that the bible teaches us that God is intent on destroying the earth and replacing it with an entirely new and pristine copy. Steve Bishop indicates how in each of the texts they use[87] there is a great deal of textual and contextual evidence to suggest that the intended emphasis is transformation rather than destruction and renewal.[88] For example, Bishop cites Tischendorf, Westcott and Hort who all insist that when we read in 2 Peter 3:10 that on the Day of the Lord 'the elements will be destroyed by fire,' a more widely attested translation of the last phrase reads 'will be found'. He also insists that Jesus' words 'Heaven and Earth will pass away' in Matthew 24:35 could just as accurately be rendered 'Heaven and Earth will be transformed' and purified by the fire. There will be no replacement because history and culture have advanced and we have developed in the way (although not always in the direction) God intended us to do. It is our mistakes and the effects of the evil we have chosen which are to be redeemed, and it is God's perfect will which is to be restored. 'The kingdom of God claims *all* of creation, not only in all its departments, but also in all its stages of development.'[88]

As Nigel Wright rightly says:

> The biblical passages which look forward to a final conflict, or a catastrophic purging of creation (see, for example, 2 Peter 3:10-11), should be understood as the action of God in removing from the creation that which does not truly belong to it. The goal of this is to produce the new heaven and earth in which all things are fully indwelt by God in Christ through the Spirit (Rev. 21).[90]

The whole earth will undergo a total restoration, and the new thing God is committed to doing has a continuity with the present earth, but also promises a change, for, 'just as our bodies will be raised imperishable for the glory of God, so the earth itself will be made new and fit for the habitation of risen and glorified persons.'[91] The fact that 'there is a real passing away, and there is a real continuity, a real connection'[92] means that there is also a real reason for prizing and treasuring the creation as God's gift until God releases creation from its purposelessness and the labour pains of creation give birth to the new heavens and earth when the present is set free from its slavery to decay.[93]

And that should not really come as any great surprise because surely this is something that both the Old Testament prophets and the Apostle John foresaw when they wrote about a future time when the earth will enjoy a heavenly peace[94] which will be matched by a restored harmony within the

161

animal kingdom and between us and the animals.[95] Until now we have had to make do with glimpses of what will become possible in the future.[96] But then, environmental harmony will be universally restored,[97] and the indication is that the restoration of the blessings of the Garden 'will match "the glorious liberty of the children of God".'[98]

But, in the meantime, the problem is so serious that it will not be solved by a wave of God's arm (however mighty that arm might be) or by human attempts to do their best to revert to correct behaviour. For, whilst it is true that confession and repentance bring about birth into a new hope in Christ, and any resulting embracing of wise 'stewardship brings liberation for nature;'[99] it will not be until God calls a halt to this wayward earth and personally restores all things to a state of inherent rightness that paradise will be regained. The coming of the Kingdom of God is also 'not yet'.

In the meantime, it is essential we affirm that

> God's love for creation takes the same form as God's love for human beings, and both the covenant love of the Old Testament and the *agape* love of the New may be applied to the entire cosmos.[100]

We have seen how Romans 8 ties up the redemption of fallen nature with the redemption of humans[101] and Paul's insistence in Colossians 1 that God's intention is to reconcile all things to himself.[102] And that should come as no surprise to us since the God of the Old Testament who gave us pictures of eschatological salvation that combined 'references to transformed persons, transformed relations between Israel and the nations, and a transformed nature.'[103] is the same God who sent his Son because he so loved the *cosmos*.[104] Thus the cross of Christ vindicates the whole creation to the extent that it undermines dualism and declares that nature is worth dying for – and has been at every point from creation to the end of time.

162

George Kehm believes that the language Paul uses in his comments on the resurrection body in 1 Corinthians 15 implies that there is an essential bond between humanity and the earth on which we live. He says that by moving from the Greek word *soma* (body v. 38) to *sarx* (flesh v. 39) Paul is declaring that the whole animal kingdom – of which we are part – shares the same kind of physical reality. Our commonality is founded upon our shared creator and is underlined by the fact that we are all perishable.[105] Kehm admits that this passage only hints that there is 'an essential bond' between us and nature, and believes that it is in Romans 8 that this bond emerges most powerfully. The linking of the present state and the future destiny of creation indicates to Kehm that 'the logic of this view of redemption is that unless redemption is cosmic, it cannot be complete for any part of the creation, not even the human part or some segment of the human part.'[106]

One of the most intriguing themes running through some recent theological works is illustrated by André Dumas and Will Hoyt who insist that the fact that humanity and nature are in relationship means that it is possible for the tables to be turned – with the possibility that the animals might have a part to play in helping us to behave with ecological wisdom. Dumas begins with the observation that 'some, however, are not convinced that the wolf is as ecologically insane as the human being,' and goes on to insist that 'what is happening today is something essentially new. In certain respects the animal kingdom is emerging as a pattern which can help man to recover his true nature.'[107] This, Dumas insists, is because the less intellectually free-ranging animal follows its instincts where we prefer to listen to our intellect or our drives for power and prestige. The animal is therefore limited in its ability to control its environment, and is more concerned about ensuring its immediate survival. This is interesting, but not very helpful since we cannot undo the way we have been created, and even if we could do so we would only be avoiding our God-given responsibilities.

I am far more challenged by Will Hoyt who, in his article *Finding God in the 'Death of Nature'*,[108] seems to echo the Revelation of the apostle John whose prophecies suggest that the end of the age will be marked by all manner of environmental catastrophes. Hoyt insists that when we watch and wait (in what he calls a 'Christian sense') we notice that the world *is* becoming a quieter place. Species, habitats and ecosystems are disappearing. The planet seems to be dying. But amidst all this death, nature still focuses upon 'a far country'; meaning that paradoxically:

> God may now be coming into better focus, through nature, than has previously been possible. For surely God, in the person of the Son, is there – dying – 'in and through' the spruces atop Mt. Mitchell in North Carolina just as he has been present in and through the suffering of all innocents since the beginning of time.[109]

Christ chose to identify himself with the state of the fallen world as he hung on the cross – and his identification is more than just sympathy.

> Looking at nature dying is like looking at the Kingdom, crucified, and I can think of no better picture of God. Conversely, it is hard to imagine any image other than crucifixion that could adequately do justice to the extent of man's hatred towards nature, and, as well, to the extent of the agony other creatures have suffered on account of that hate. In other words, the death of nature – should it occur – would be a profoundly revelatory event.[110]

It is now that God's covenant with creation, our joint experience of the Fall and Paul's hope that the whole creation will share the freedom of Christ's victory begin to form a harmonious unit. For although Hoyt shares Lynn White's fascination with St Francis of Assisi, he approves of Francis because he embraced a lifestyle which indicated an appreciation of the link between mankind and nature which is only revealed to most of us when 'Sister Earth' is enveloped by 'Sister Death'.[111] Could it really be true that nature's suffering was taken into Christ when he was crucified? It would certainly not be out of character for a God who delights to reveal himself as a vulnerable lamb being sacrificed for the sins of the world.

If Hoyt is right, then he is saying something of equal importance when he comments:

> Somehow or other we have just got to get it into our heads that when we see a dying wood we are in fact seeing a very fountain of life – an aspect of that moment 2000 years ago when Life itself was broken in order that the rest of us (sparrows, people, whales) might live. For if we don't learn to see in this strange 'new' way, if we don't overcome our habitual linkage of the beautiful and good solely to that which is pristine and inviolate, we will have done nothing to overcome our plunder-and-move-on ethic.[112]

I cannot help but see Hoyt's article as a kind of commentary upon chapters 8 and 9 of the Book of Revelation in which we are presented with seven trumpets of warning. Although John does not interpret these images for us, the fact that they include burned earth, destroyed trees, shrivelled vegetation, barren seas and poisoned rivers should make us sit up and wonder what God is teaching us about our ability to govern the earth without the benefit of his guiding presence. The end of chapter 9 underlines the fact that the death of nature is indissolubly linked to the death of morality and our determination to resist God. 'All of which is to say, nature isn't dead any more than we are. To the extent that we harden our hearts, nature dies. To the extent that we lift up our hearts and allow God entrance, nature lives.'[113]

Surely this is the lesson that nature is trying to teach us. So:

those of us who worry about the fate of the earth have got it exactly backwards. 'Save the whales,' everyone is always saying . . . 'Save the wolf'. But in the end the wolves are already saved. Or rather, they have never been in danger of being lost. For *they are who they're called to be.*[114]

This need not underplay their solidarity with us in our fallen state, and neither does it mean that the suffering of a whale or a wolf is unimportant, or even that it is not scandalous, but:

if other creatures could speak they would tell us to worry for ourselves rather than for streams or wolves or spotted owls. Like Jesus they would tell us that, if only we had ears to hear, the Kingdom of Heaven is within us, not just outside us, and that nature suffers chiefly to the extent that we, unlike all other creatures, don't yet allow that kingdom to take root in the soil of our hearts. They would tell us, in effect, that they were – as Paul says – 'waiting.' They would tell us that nature was to be raised as a whole and that the only thing wanting was for as many of us who are called to be adopted as daughters and sons.[115]

In this sense it is right that the Christian religion is human centred – it is us who are called to repent and return to God because it was us who fell. We need to return to God and relearn how to be humble servants in order that we might learn to live and let others live too. This does not make us more important than the rest of creation, it simply reflects the fact that to those whom God gives more, much more is expected. After all, it is not the rest of creation which has hardened itself against God. The whole of nature will be redeemed, of that there is no doubt. But as it waits, it is part of God's 'megaphone to rouse a deaf world'[116] and implore humanity to obey God and live.

So, in the end, what we have in scripture is a promise that in reconciling all things to Christ, God is providing the basis whereby all things can also be reconciled to each other. The final aim of God is:

to communicate his life to another in a way which calls forth at the very end new heavens and a new earth in which righteousness dwells, a transfigured cosmos where peace is universally established between all creatures at last, in the midst of which is situated a glorious city of resurrected saints who dwell in justice, blessed with all the resplendent fullness of the earth, and who continually call upon all creatures to join with them in their joyful praise of the one who is all in all.[117]

Or as John Piper says:

So history as we know it will come to an end with God at the center. His glory will be so bright as to make a moon out of the sun (Revelation 21:23). And on the earth there will be a great sea of knowledge reflecting the glory of the Lord back to him. And just as the rejection of that knowledge brought a curse on the creation, so the restoration of that knowledge will bring blessing to the creation, and the animals themselves with be free from the curse and reflect the beauty of the Lord.[118]

In the meantime, as we wait and anticipate the return of the Christ who will make all things new, God calls us to respond appropriately to the calls of his groaning creation. The final thing I want to do is look at how we might take appropriate action, but first, since God-directed action is mediated to us as we rest, listen, and worship we pray:

Father in Heaven
it is time you came. For our time is running out
and our world is passing away.
You gave us our life with one another.
We have wrecked it by declaring war against one another.
You gave us trees and forests.
We have cut them down.
To the bird you gave the spring
and to the fish the rivers.
We have silenced the spring and polluted the rivers.
To the work of your creation

you gave balance.
We have upset it and therefore come to grief.
Come, Creator of all,
renew the lifeless face of the earth.
Despite our unhappiness
give us hope for your Day
when, at peace with every creature,
we can laugh and praise you.[119]

Notes

1. Richard Syms – *The Ferris Wheel. Searching for an Adult Faith.* (SCM. London. 1988) p 23.
2. Compare Genesis 3:15 and Colossians 2:15.
3. Genesis 3:21.
4. Genesis 4:15.
5. John Ziesler. *Paul's Letter to the Romans* (SCM. London. 1989) p 219.
6. Deiter Hessel – 'Eco-Justice Theology After Nature's Revolt.' This article forms the introduction to *After Nature's Revolt. Eco-Justice and Theology.* Ed. Hessel (Fortress Press, Minneapolis, Minnesota. 1992) p 15.
7. See Matthew 25:34-46 and Luke 10:25-37.
8. John Cobb Jr. – 'Postmodern Christianity in Quest of Eco-Justice.' in Hessel. op. cit. (1992) p 24.
9. Romans 8:14-16 and 23.
10. Matthew 12:28.
11. Colossians 1:13.
12. George Zerbe – 'The Kingdom of God and the Stewardship of Creation.' in DeWitt (ed.) *The Environment and the Christian: What does the New Testament say about the Environment?* (Baker Book House. Grand Rapids, Michigan. 1991) p 83.
13. Wolters – *Creation Regained.* (Eerdmans. Grand Rapids. Michigan. 1992) p 64-69.
14. Ibid. p 65.
15. Ibid.
16. Patrick Nullens – *Leven volgens Gaia's normen? De verhouding tussen God, mens en aarde, en de implicaties voor ecologische ethiek.* Doctoral Thesis for the Evangelische Theologische Faculteit. p 334.
17. Matthew 11:12; 12:28-29; Luke 10:18; 17:21.
18. Romans 8:14.
19. Ziesler. op. cit. (1989) p 219.
20. 2 Peter 3:13; Revelation 21:1-4.
21. Jürgen Moltmann – *Theology of Hope. On the grounds and implications of a Christian Eschatology.* – (SCM. London. 1967)
22. Ibid. p 103.

23. Bauckham – *Moltmann: Messianic Theology in the Making*. (Marshall Pickering. Basingstoke. 1987) p 85. See also p 86.
24. Ibid. p 88-90.
25. Moltmann. op. cit. (1967) p 172-82.
26. Bauckham. op. cit. (1987) p 36.
27. Moltmann. op. cit. (1967) p 211.
28. Bauckham. op. cit. p 36. (italics mine)
29. Moltmann. op. cit. (1967) p 221.
30. Which Moltmann believes is clearly distinguishable from the spirit of utopia because it is grounded in the person and history of Jesus Christ. (op. cit. (1967) p 17)
31. Ibid. p 337-8.
32. Bauckham. op. cit. (1987) p 42.
33. Ibid. p 10.
34. Ibid. p 124.
35. Which Moltmann calls *'futurum'* – meaning that certain visions of the future can be extrapolated from the past and the present.
36. Moltmann calls these unseen potentialities *'adventus'*. reflecting the fact that the coming of such a future can only be known by prophetic anticipation. (see Bauckham. op. cit. (1987) p 43.)
37. White – 'Historical Roots' *Science* 10 March 1967 Vol. 155 No 3767. op. cit. p 1206. White paints a picture of the Western saint as one who is typified by his penchant for action in place of contemplation.
38. Moltmann – *God in Creation*. (SCM. London. 1985)
39. Ibid. p 276.
40. Ibid. p 279.
41. This is the same 'relationship' that we saw at the beginning of Part Two.
42. Moltmann – op. cit. (1985) p 280.
43. Meaning that God set it apart or sanctified it.
44. Exodus 20:8-11.
45. Moltmann. op. cit. (1985) p 285.
46. Ibid. p 286.
47. Leviticus 25:1-7.
48. Leviticus 25:8-55.
49. Moltmann. op. cit. (1985) p 288.
50. Romans 8:18.
51. Ziesler. op. cit. p 219.
52. Moltmann. op. cit. (1985) p 288.
53. I use the term 'cosmological dualism' to distinguish it from the nine other types N.T. Wright describes in his book *The New Testament and the People of God*. (SPCK. London. 1992) p 252-4. By it I mean the dualism inherent in Plato who views the material world as a shadow of the real spiritual world which can only be understood by the mind of the 'enlightened'.

54. John Cobb Jr. – 'Postmodern Christianity in quest of Eco-justice.' in Hessel op. cit. (1992) p 22.

55. Dispensationalism is a branch of Pre-Millennial thought which considers that it is possible to split the whole of the period of the bible up into distinct periods during which God deals differently with his people. The movement is characterized by extreme pessimism and the belief that it is not possible for humans to create any lasting peace or justice because of our sinfulness. They look forward to the final Millennial age when Christ will reign on the earth; believing that the earth as it is stands condemned by God and it is of little value to talk of saving it from the destruction which it merits and which will inaugurate Christ's second coming.

56. George Tinker – 'Creation as Kin. An American Indian view.' in Hessel op. cit. (1992) p 151.

57. This includes a commitment to Eco-Justice. Dieter Hessel defines the main tenets of this strand of justice in the introduction to his book – and they mirror many of the themes we considered in the first part of this study.

58. John Cobb Jr. – 'Postmodern Christianity' Hessel. op. cit. (1992) p 24.

59. 2 Corinthians 5:18, 19. According to the longer ending of Mark's Gospel this good news is to be preached to all creation.

60. Colossians 3:9b-10. See also 1 Corinthians 11:7.

61. 1 Corinthians 15:45.

62. 2 Corinthians 4:4-6; Colossians 1:15.

63. Romans 5:17. See also verses 18 and 19.

64. Moltmann. op. cit. (1985) p 226.

65. Romans 8:29.

66. Moltmann. op. cit. (1985) p 226.

67. Colossians 1:16-17.

68. Ronald Manahan – 'Christ as the Second Adam.' in Calvin DeWitt (ed.) – *The Environment and the Christian. What can we learn from the New Testament?* op. cit. (1991) p 51-2.

69. We have already seen this in a slightly different situation – where disobedience is linked with God's curse upon the land (e.g. Deut. 28:30-40)

70. Romans 12:2.

71. Matthew 5:17-18.

72. Susan P. Bratton – 'Loving Nature. Eros or Agape?' in *Environmental Ethics.* Spring 1992. Vol. 14. No 1.

73. Bratton defines Eros as 'love of beauty or natural (including sexual and romantic) love with a desire to possess.'

74. Ibid. p 5.

75. Bratton defines Agape as 'Godly love or sacrificial love.'

76. Bratton. ibid. p 25.

77. 1 John 4:7-16.

78. Anne Primavesi – 'The Part for the Whole. An Ecofeminist Enquiry.' in *Theology.* Vol. XCIII. No 755. SPCK. September 1990. p 355.

79. Primavesi. ibid. p 356.
80. Catherina Halkes. New Creation. *Christian Feminism and the Renewal of the Earth* (SPCK. London. 1997) p 22f.
81. Both of which are thought of as passive conquests and desired by men as possessions to dis-cover. The association of women with nature and men with culture is explored in some depth in Halkes. op. cit. Chapter 1.
82. Primavesi. op. cit. (1990) p 356.
83. Mary Grey – *The Wisdom of Fools: Seeking Revelation for Today.* (SPCK. London. 1993) p 18-20.
84. For example the shift towards urbanism and the false division of reality into 'sacred' and 'secular' compartments.
85. Ibid.
86. Ibid. p 359.
87. See Matthew 24:35; 2 Peter 3:10-13; Hebrews 1:12.
88. Bishop – 'Green Theology and Deep Ecology.' *Thermelios* April/May 1991 Vol. 16 No 3 p 10.
89. Ibid. p 64.
90. Nigel Wright – *Challenge to Change: A Radical Agenda for Baptists.* (Kingsway. Eastbourne. 1991) p 41.
91. John Piper – *Future Grace.* (IVP. Leicester. 1995) p 374.
92. Piper. op. cit. (1995) p 376.
93. These images are taken from the Good News rendering of Romans 8:20-21.
94. Isaiah 2:4; Micah 4:3.
95. Isaiah 11:6-8; 65:25.
96. The lives of Jesus (see Mark 1:13) and Francis of Assisi seem the best examples.
97. Isaiah 35:6, 7 and Revelation 21:1-4.
98. Ziesler. op. cit. (1992) p 221.
99. Bishop 'Green Theology and Deep Ecology.' op. cit. p 9.
100. Bratton. 'Loving Nature, Eros or Agape?' op. cit. p 24.
101. See for example. Gulick – The Bible and Ecological Spirituality *Theology Today* July 1991. p 191. and Bishop. op. cit. (1991) p 10.
102. We cannot restrict 'all things' to human creation alone since in this context 'ta panta' is defined as 'all things on earth and in heaven'.
103. George Kehm – 'The New Story. Redemption as Fulfilment of Creation.' in Hessel. op. cit. (1992) p 96.
104. John 3:16.
105. Kehm. op. cit. p 101-2.
106. Ibid. p 102.
107. André Dumas – 'The Ecological Crisis and the Doctrine of Creation.' *The Ecumenical Review.* Vol. XXVII. No 1. January 1975. WCC. p 30.
108. Will Hoyt – 'Finding God in the Death of Nature.' in *New Oxford Review.* July/August 1991.

109. Hoyt. ibid. p 7-8.
110. Ibid. p 8.
111. These images are taken from St Francis' prayer entitled 'The Canticle of the Sun.'
112. Hoyt. op. cit. (1991) p 9.
113. Ibid. p 10.
114. Ibid.
115. Ibid.
116. This is an image which is used (of the phenomenon of pain) by C.S. Lewis in *The Problem of Pain*. (The Centenary Press. London. 1941) p 81.
117. Santmire – *The Travail of Nature*. (Fortress Press. Minneapolis, Minnesota. 1985) p 217-8.
118. John Piper. *Future Grace*. (IVP. Leicester. 1995) p 379.
119. Published anonymously in D. Cremer – *Sing me the Song of my World*. (St Paul Publications. Slough. 1981) p 140-1.

CHAPTER FIVE

~

Harvest:
The Festival of Creation

What does a Creation Festival look like?

The beginning of the Third Millennium is a fitting time to take a long look at the world we have created, and begin to repent of our failures to steward the earth as we should have done. It is also important that we see our failures in the context of scripture because through it God seems to be speaking the words 'I told you so' into our present predicament and he waits for humanity to respond by returning to him in penitence. Many readers will have got this far and may still be asking 'So what? Where is the call for the kind of action that will make a positive difference to creation and begin to turn things around?' This is a fair response, because if creation's waiting in Romans 8 has a present dimension, and if Christians are called to be Priests and responsible stewards, our response must be more earthy – more practical. It is my firm belief that Christians need to hear the cries of the whale and the wolf. We must hear them and respond. But how?

The hope of redemption fixes our eyes upon two points of future promise. The first thing it calls us to do is to lift our gaze to a distant horizon. We need to see where God is taking us so that we will be prevented from expending time and energy working against the grain of creation's future history. We also need to be encouraged to see that there is a future to be working towards, and that any efforts we take in trying to co-operate with the Lord of Creation will be well spent. Too much of our new-found environmental concern encourages us to worry, react and panic – all in response to a vision of the future in which there is no future – unless we create it for ourselves.

175

The Christian must recognize that the earth is not out of control even when we believe it to be out of our control. This means that there is no need for us to run around like headless chickens trying to save the world from destruction, but it need not mean that the future we have created for ourselves is to be bright and rosy.

The Christian gains true perspective by resting and listening to God. This is the lesson of the Sabbath which is about both enjoyment and observation of the inherent goodness and vitality of creation. This does not mean that activity is forbidden, but it guards us against the kind of panic which breeds fear and makes activity unproductive. The future has a certainty to it that serves as a calming influence and gives us the confidence that says: 'it is worth going on.' If 'Eat, drink and be merry, for tomorrow we die' is not a Christian option; neither is 'Hurry, let's do X, Y and Z *so that* tomorrow we will not die.'

Do not misunderstand me. I am not suggesting for one minute that the Christian should not be active in caring for the environment – the hope of redemption not only makes it possible for the 'sons of God' to be enactors of the demands of justice and stewardship, but renders responsible action a Christian imperative. Nor am I suggesting that only Christians can care for the environment properly, and that we should be forming Christian organizations to mirror the work of the many environmental campaign and research groups. *Humans* are created in the image of God, and *humans* are told to be stewards of creation. The fact that non-Christians, who may not recognize or value the image of God within them, are recognizing and responding to God's demands without acknowledging the presence of the God who issues them is to their credit. The fact that the passion for justice and wise stewardship is far greater in many who know little of the bible than it is amongst many Christians is indicative of just how disobedient those who know God have been.

Surely God is using men and women created in his image to form organizations like Friends of the Earth, Greenpeace and many others. Such groups are concerned about issues that are close to God's heart, and the questions they ask and the things they do reflect a longing for the coming kingdom of God. But those who do not possess the Holy Spirit nor submit themselves to his rule can never be prophets who see the whole picture. Christians are called to stand in the gap and supplement this prophetic action and passion for justice with their own unique contributions: faith, hope for the future and worshipful obedience to the creator.

But, for many Christians, caring for creation is still seen as a fringe issue. Why? I have already suggested a number of answers, all of which contribute to the problem: we are steeped in Greek thought and have the mistaken view that it is Christian. Prominent Christians have taught that God has given nature to us and allowed us to use it as we see fit. The Fall has so damaged us and our relationship with creation that we have come to believe that we have no choice but to dominate it. We are so caught up in the material progress of mankind that it has become our all-consuming passion and we have come to believe that we live in a human centred, material universe.

These are some of the reasons, and I could go on. But, in truth, they are only excuses; because all this time we have had the bible, with its story of creation, its laws and its warnings. The only thing that is different about today is that as we look around us and see what we have done to our world, and as we recognize that much of the devastation we witness has come to us because of our own actions, we are becoming worried – for our own survival. It is only now that Christians are beginning to open themselves to the word of God in a new way. When God's warnings seemed a distant threat and could be put off, we ignored them. But now they are close to home, and we are concerned to discover what we can do to put things right. And so today we are interested to rediscover the wisdom and the insights which have been lost to the Christian tradition for so long: for all those years when mankind thought God's rules were unduly restrictive and the giver of them was miserly.

In our existential age, we find it hard to conceive of law as something positive – beyond the obvious fact that it restricts evil. But the law of the Old Testament was a framework which, when God's people lived by it, was recognized as a mediator of great blessing – because it was rooted in a covenant with a loving and a generous God. So Old Testament law is not a series of arbitrary restrictions, but is all about recreating a system of right relationships which are founded upon a firm footing. The law is based upon an acceptance of the seriousness of sin and the provision of sacrifices which remove guilt and alienation from God. But this is not a solemn affair in the way we think of legal restrictions. The law of God is all about freedom from sin and the enjoyment of a relationship with God. It is no surprise then that in the midst of the Old Testament law we find a succession of invitations to feasts and parties, each of which are intended as annual reminders of God's past goodness and promises of his continuing faithfulness if his worshippers remained obedient. The main festivals are set out in Leviticus 23, repeated in greater detail in Numbers 28 and 29, and will prove to be our passport to practical action.

The Passover commemorated deliverance from Egypt. The people rested for seven days and ate only unleavened bread as a reminder of their flight. In Leviticus 23, verses 9-13 God reminds his people that when they took possession of the land he had promised them they were to make him a special offering of a loaf of bread made from the first batch of grain they harvested, a male lamb, flour, olive oil and wine. These offerings were to ensure that God would accept them, and were to be repeated 'for all time to come'.

Two months after the Passover came the Feast of Weeks (seven weeks after the first harvest) or Pentecost. This was a kind of Harvest Festival. Again, a further offering of corn was presented to God, along with more bread made from the first harvest, a number of lambs and goats and a quantity of wine. God also demanded that this festival was to be repeated each year, and he followed his instructions with the command that when harvesting his fields, the farmer was to leave the corn at the edges of the field and only harvest it once – so that the poor and the foreigners could eat the grain that remained.

The next festival in the calendar was the New Year feast, in which the people would gather together for worship, blow trumpets and present a food offering to God. The occasion was also a rest day from work. This was followed by the Day of Atonement at which there would be a sacrifice for sin and God would forgive his people. Again, a food offering was to be made and no work was to be done, but this time the people were also to fast as a sign of humility and repentance.

Finally came the Feast of Tabernacles or Booths, which was a seven day festival marking the end of harvest and recalling the time Israel lived in the wilderness before they entered the promised land. In addition to rest and worship the people were also expected to bring the best of all types of crops as a thank offering to God for a good harvest.

Each of these five festivals were similar to the Sabbath, in as far as these times were set aside for rest, worship and celebration, and were opportunities to acknowledge God as their provider and deliverer. These would be festivals of heartfelt celebration and were opportunities for the whole of Israel to express their devotion to the God who had blessed them so richly. It was also a time when they were to make their offerings to God and rededicate themselves to the covenant. If, for any reason, someone was excluded from the feast it was a time of great disappointment.[1]

These times of celebration were set like pearls right at the heart of the law. The intention was that by setting time aside for worship, the festivals were to serve as seasonal reminders of the fact that God had placed himself right at the heart of the Israelite community, and that his intention was to bless his people, and through them bring blessing to his wayward world. The joy and splendour of each occasion was meant to guard against the law becoming cold and lifeless and was designed to help the people of God see it as a law of love which guarded their precious relationship with their deliverer. These feasts were important reminders to Israel of their national and spiritual identity. But time and again the people either failed to observe them, or they performed the outward ritual of the festival and forgot its true meaning. Each time this happened, and sinful human nature had its way, God would call his people back to true and faithful obedience.[2]

The law and the Old Testament Covenant were God's responses to sin, and pointed to both his grace and justice. They also foresaw a time when God would set his people free from the shackles of having to obey written laws to please him, since they looked forward to a time when he would write his law on their hearts, and God himself would dwell with his people. So with the coming of Jesus – God's Messiah – the Old Covenant was replaced with the New, and the requirements of the law, although still valid ways of pleasing God, were superseded by the new thing God was doing in Christ. So although Jesus observed these festivals and the early church seems to have continued celebrating them,[3] it did not take long for the Christian church to adopt its own calendar to take account of New Testament theology and the need to celebrate this using new symbols. So the Passover lamb becomes the body of Christ and is celebrated at the time we now know as Easter; The Day of Atonement can perhaps be equated with the Lord's supper: our frequent reminder of the events of Good

Friday and Easter Sunday; the Sabbath becomes Sunday; the Feast of Weeks was the inspiration behind Lammas; and the Day of Trumpets loses its religious significance and is mirrored by our national celebration of New Year.

Festivals shaped Hebrew life since they helped to integrate the spiritual life of the nation with everyday events. The modified Christian festivals of the early Church continued this pattern; but by the Middle Ages the church calendar year degenerated into a farce – with such a variety of feast days and Saints' days that those events which carried the greatest theological significance became choked by the undergrowth. Feasts and festivals largely lost their meaning and became times for superstitious appeasement rather than true celebratory events. By the time of the Reformation many of the Protestant reformers responded to this widespread abuse of the festivals by dropping everything. So Jean Calvin scrapped the entire church calendar, and in the next century the Puritans even refused to celebrate Christmas. Thus today there is no such thing as common practice in the celebration of feast days and festivals – even within the established denominations. I confess that I have never been keen on calendar worship in the past – mainly because they tend to be the times of year when people who cling to traditions demand that things are done in ways they have always been done in the past, and my nature is always to be looking for new and relevant ways to express old truths to those who have become alienated by the traditions of the Church. But on reflection it has become clear that it is not the festivals themselves that I object to, but the misuse of them. My mind is now changing because I have become convinced that festival times are important reminders that theology is not primarily a cerebral event. If it is to be alive and bring life it must lead to worship and response.

Festivals are vital because they serve as important reminders of key truths and core Christian values. So whilst the replacement of Old Testament festivals with Christian symbols was both natural and important, it is my firm belief that the secularization of the Day of Trumpets, the decline of Lammas and the Harvest festival and the fact that in recent decades we have become distanced from the processes of agriculture which has become increasingly mechanized and dependent upon far fewer people; has had a significant impact upon the way we now view the creation. In the Old Testament, the Day of Trumpets came to be associated with God's work of creation and his judgement; the Feasts of Weeks and Tabernacles both placed important emphases upon the goodness of creation and upon social justice and stewardship; and Harvest was the time of thanksgiving for another completed agricultural cycle.

Previous generations were more in touch with the soil than we are, and also enjoyed a greater number of agricultural services found within their Christian calendar. By the Nineteenth Century there were four such services: Plough Sunday, Rogation, Lammas and Harvest.[4]

Plough Sunday

In early and Medieval times the church was the place where the communal plough was kept. Plough Sunday was introduced during Victorian times, was celebrated on the first Sunday after Epiphany, and marked the return to work after the Christmas break. It was the time to celebrate the goodness of the land and the miracle of growth, and of honouring the task of the winter feeding of cattle. It was also the time of looking ahead to the long process of preparing the ground for the seed.

Rogation Sunday

Rogation Sunday was celebrated on the fifth Sunday after Easter, at a time when the earth was visibly undergoing renewal. The background to this day was that it was originally the time when the people asked the Holy Spirit to help them be true sons of God (*rogare* being Latin for 'to ask'). However, in the 1630s, the poet George Herbert commended the twin rogation themes of seeking God's blessing on the fields and marking the boundaries of the land. Herbert was concerned that this was to be the time when walking the bounds together enabled neighbours to reconcile their differences and the poor were helped by those with enough. Prior to Rogation Sunday, Rogation days were held on the first three days of the week preceding Ascension Sunday and were developed from the Roman rites of Robigalia (*robigo* being Latin for 'mould' or 'rust'), when God would be asked to protect the crops from mildew.

Lammas

Lammas and the Harvest festival are the most biblical of agricultural festivals. Lammas was celebrated on August 1st and paralleled the Old Testament Feast of Weeks or First Fruits. The word comes either from lamb-mass or loaf-mass, and it was customary for each celebrant to offer that which was appropriate to their situation. Like the Old Testament feast, it was an opportunity to affirm that honouring God came first in the order of priorities.

The Harvest Festival

Harvest is really the only creation-care festival that still survives as a popular Christian worship occasion. But even then I should qualify that statement since I am in danger of making a huge generalization. We live in a world of tremendous variety – and the Christian Church is no different. Some churches choose to make a big thing about Harvest, whilst others refer to it almost in passing or forget it altogether. Whilst Harvest is relatively popular, it is also undergoing a slow decline. The pattern of many surviving Harvest Services is derived from a form of service established over a century ago by Parson

Hawker of Morwenstow in Cornwall. But this form of Harvest is no longer a festival that catches the imagination. In recent generations the Christian Harvest Festival has followed the pattern of this book. In the past, Harvest was a time of full churches and impressive displays of produce. As a celebration it was full of meaning and life. But it has undergone a catastrophic fall – partly as a long-term result of the loss of the focus provided by the other feasts, and also because most people in our modern world have less contact with the land than they did in previous generations. Consequently our Harvest festival has all too often become an event which is rarely celebrated by anyone outside the church because it has not evolved to take account of this rapidly changing world. Even to those inside the church it is all too often reduced to little more than a collection of a few bags of garden produce, a pile of tins from the supermarket, and heaps of wilting vegetation from the hedgerows, and the true meaning of the festival has become lost under the rapidly diminishing heaps of produce.

I believe that the decline of Harvest is a sign that over the years it has become detached from its theological foundations, and from the real lives of most people in our modern industrialized societies. In many places the idea of offering to God became superseded by the tradition of producing a harvest display. But the two are, actually, very different. Perhaps we have also failed to recognize the full impact of the fact that most people no longer grow their own food. The vast majority of the foodstuffs we eat have been grown by other people, often in other countries, and arrive at our tables via supermarkets or corner shops. This means that, practically speaking, we have arrived at the point where we take the fruitfulness of the soil under our feet for granted. Thus we find it hard to see how the themes of Plough Sunday, Rogation, Lammas and Harvest touch our lives. So, not only have we lost contact with the earth we have been instructed to tend and become independent from the point of production, but we have also become unconcerned about how others treat it so long as that land does not belong to us, and we get the food we want to eat.

The economic reality of our modern world is that the West has evolved into a collection of technological and service-based economies. Agricultural services were last promoted after World War Two when the older rural ways seemed under threat from an urbanized culture. In recent years the agricultural festivals have declined as a focus of worship, and the majority of us have become alienated from the land. At the same time much of the Western world has also become both greedy and complacent. I am convinced that these two facts are not unconnected. Water hoses irrigate the land, genetic engineering and pesticides ensure healthy crops, fertilizers encourage increased fruitfulness, and favourable trade arrangements ensure we get the variety of food we require at the prices we are prepared to pay. So even Harvest has become an outmoded festival, and it is a secularized version of Christmas that has become the season which captures both the imagination and the spirit of the age. This is because we have lost touch with who we are, and have become unable to enjoy the good gifts God has given us without feeling we have to both own and control them.

But the time has come to challenge this state of affairs, and I suggest that the way to do this is to renew Harvest and make it into our new creation care festival. I suggest Harvest as opposed to the other three for two reasons. The first is that it still retains a relative popularity, and the second is that since it is the festival which is enjoyed as a consequence of caring for creation it will be possible to focus on issues of stewardship from the perspectives of both worship and wisdom – meaning that we can use the occasion to look back and learn from both our successes and failures to steward the earth as God intends. I believe that in the current Post-modern climate in which there is little concensus about whether there is any such thing as absolute truth, the most powerful lessons will have to be learned through evaluating consequences rather than spending much time debating the value of differing ethical prescriptions – although this will have to result in an appreciation that there are some non-negotiable absolutes if we are to avoid the process of endlessly repeating the mistakes of the past. But if we are to use Harvest we will need to incorporate the lessons of Plough, Rogation and Lammas, whilst also making the festival more relevant to a world which has entered the twenty-first century. I am convinced that if we succeed in doing this, we will discover that Harvest is the ideal vehicle for putting the Christian emphasis upon creation care back at the centre of Christian theology where it can then have a meaningful impact on our world which so longs to be reunited with itself. In order to do this we will need to look a little more closely at the Old Testament texts, and then translate what we find there into ideas and symbols which speak to the needs of our modern world.

The Meaning of Harvest

In Deuteronomy 26 we find a parallel passage to Leviticus 23. This chapter anticipates the entry into Canaan, and is written to catalogue 'the ideal response which the worshipper is to make'[5] when coming into God's presence at the first Festival of Weeks. The passage highlights a number of important features which underlie this important festival. The words the worshipper is instructed to use place him in no doubt that at the centre of the harvest festival comes the recognition that the fruitful land that has produced its crops in such abundance has been given to him and his fellow worshippers by God. The most immediate implication of this is the reminder that the soil which produced the crops also belongs to God. But land also had social, psychological and religious value for each member of the community, and still does today. Thus land is part of our lives, it is tied up with our security and sense of belonging and is the foundation of community life and identity. So land is more than just an economic unit or a provider of a healthy return on investment, because it is essential to the healthy functioning of society. The social value of land is underlined by the Jubilee provisions in Leviticus 25, where God directs that every 50 years it was to be returned to its original owner, and in the intervening period that owner had the right to buy it back if he had the financial means to do so. The fact underlying all these rules is that 'your land must not be sold on a permanent basis, because you do not own it; it belongs to God, and you are like foreigners who are allowed to make use of it.'[6]

Thus God refuses to allow his people to see land value solely in terms of the income it produces, or the money it can be sold for. Jubilee forbids us to consider land in these terms because it is not something that can be possessed. Thus human ownership of land does not carry any absolute rights, but comes with obligations and responsibilities. In fact, it is probably not even helpful to think in terms of ownership at all. A far more useful idea is the notion of land as an inheritance: recalling the fact that it has had a past and also has a future. Each tract of land was an inheritance from God, and was received as the result of a promise. It would have been passed on by familial ancestors, and was going to be inherited by future generations. This gave an important incentive to a family to use the land responsibly, and maintained the wider family as a cohesive social unit.

As part of the law, the Jubilee directives also embody a concern for justice. The Jubilee restrictions recognize that there will be a tendency for the economically adept or powerful members of the community to prosper – whether by virtue of natural skill or through sheer hard work. And at the same time other families will fall on hard times and have to sell land in order to get by; or they will not be able to farm the land they occupy. In these cases the law allows land to be sold, and even permits a person to sell himself to another countryman – although not as a slave, but as one with the status of a hired worker or temporary resident. During this time, the one who has sold himself has the right to remain in his own country, is protected from usurers and is allowed to buy food at cost price. Every fifty years the Israelites were commanded to celebrate a year of Jubilee – during which the land is allowed to remain fallow and everyone is instructed to return to the property which God gave each family on moving into Canaan. It is not hard to see how the purpose of Jubilee is to limit greed and provide a structure of social justice whereby the rights of every individual are protected. Without such rules humans living in a post-Fall world have a tendency to dominate each other and to accumulate land. Without Jubilee there is nothing to stop the rich getting richer at the expense of the poor, and the structure of society changing so as to absolutize these structural injustices and make it impossible for the poor to get access to the land to which they have farming rights. The laws of Jubilee were never enacted for any long period of time, and this latter scenario is indeed the result we see played out in both our national and international life.

The foundation of these Jubilee laws is seen in the words the worshipper is instructed to use on bringing his gift to the Temple. Each person was instructed to recall the fact that his ancestors had once had no country in which to live, no rights and no freedom. This reminder of the past was not only a call to worship and a prompt to the people to bring their offerings, but God also expected this memory to provoke his people to live generously – sharing the fruits of their land with all who had need. When God commands: 'the Levites and the aliens

188

among you shall rejoice in all the good things the Lord your God has given to you and your household.'[7] he is reminding his people that once they had nothing of their own to offer, but now they have been given a land which does not belong to them. God is the owner, and he commands his people to share its goodness with the Levites because they were their spiritual servants and had no land and no time to grow their own crops; and with those among them who are in the same position as they used to be before their deliverance.

This land God had placed his people in was, by all accounts, extremely fertile.[8] William Dumbrell lists the features of the land they were to inherit and says:

> from a covenantal point of view, the implications of all this are as important as they are obvious. One can hardly escape the impression that what is being depicted through such references is Eden recaptured, paradise recovered.[9]

Dumbrell goes on to suggest that it is this high calling that makes the law so important, for without it their occupation of the promised land would be as temporary as Eden had been. The blessings of the garden had been surrendered, but the fruit of the promised land was the creator's way of giving blessing back to his people in a way that would not enable them to claim any credit, or assume that it was their legitimate right. God is giving Israel the opportunity to enjoy 'the gifts of creation in the way in which they had [been] meant to be used.'[10] And the only way it becomes possible to enjoy the gifts of creation rightly is when we allow ourselves to rest – which, we recall, was the purpose of the Sabbath; and is also a prime foundation of the festivals, the Sabbath year and Jubilee.

> In this theology of rest we are clearly returning to the purposes of creation set forth in Genesis 1:1-2.4a and typified by the Eden narrative, namely that mankind was created to rejoice before the

189

deity and to enjoy the blessings of creation in the divine presence.[11]

In Deuteronomy the writer seems 'very conscious of the need to underscore the fact that "rest" can be a secure doctrine only if it is tied to the correct notion of how the presence of Yahweh in the land is to be understood and appreciated.'[12] Rest is for the whole community – humans, land and animals. It is part of God's blessing upon his creation, and is an element which our profit-based and work-centred society needs to recover if we are ever to fully appreciate the good things God has given us and find the time to worship our creator as we were created to do. Rest is not defined as 'rest from work', but is given so that we may then do our work from the new perspective that rest brings.

It seems that the Old Testament Harvest celebrations have a great deal to teach us. Firstly, they are rooted in the law of God which is concerned about land, wealth, production and distribution. The Old Testament festivals of First Fruits and Harvest were also about recognizing God as the owner and ruler of this physical world, and twice yearly reminders that before we are tempted to claim anything as ours and for us to use as we see fit, we should acknowledge him as the owner and giver of everything. The people of Israel were also encouraged to recognize that since God was the owner of their land, and had given it to them, they should be prepared to use the fruit of the land for the benefit of others. This was not an option, but was included as part of the law, and was an essential prerequisite to future bountiful harvests. The festivals themselves focused upon making offerings back to God – not as a harvest display – but as a payment due to God as owner. It might be helpful to see this offering as a kind of tax; but if we do, we must guard against seeing any festival as a legalistic requirement through which we merit God's approval, or assuming that God requires a certain proportion to be given to him and the rest is ours to use as we like. The spirit of Harvest is only fully appreciated when we realize that it is a divine law – one which is fulfilled when it takes place as a true act of worship and in a spirit of celebration and joy. It is only then that we will be set free to enjoy creation and to serve it as God intended.

A New Harvest

Underlying the whole of scripture is a vision of *shalom*: peace, wholeness and a new relationship with God. Sin is the enemy of *shalom* because it encourages us to become obsessed with self, with desires to possess and with selfish ambition. And when sin reigns, and everyone does as he sees fit,[13] the beautifully intricate inter-relationships which God has woven into the fabric of creation become fractured; and we each lose our sense of the whole, and are unable to appreciate our rightful position in the created world.

In the Old Testament, God guarded us against this loss of balance by giving the Law and the Covenant. Admittedly, it was given to ancient Israel, but God's purpose was that in choosing a nation and blessing it; the surrounding nations, and ultimately the whole earth, would be drawn to return to him.[14] In a similar way God reserves the right to speak prophetically to his church in order that our response should have the same effect upon those who are not yet his. But Israel chose instead to try and keep God's blessing to themselves, whilst also refusing to follow God in any consistent way. We are faced with the same choice today.

In the New Testament, God sends his son with the same mission – to take away the sin of the world[15] and demonstrate the Father's love to the whole universe.[16] This time God places his law in the hearts of each of his redeemed people, and fills the world with his witnesses whom he directs to be salt and light to this dying and dark world. We are therefore called to be good news to a world that is lost; but are all too often unaware of why God's news is good, and what it calls us to become. Part of the reason for this is that our faith has become excessively individualistic, and like Israel we prefer to keep it to ourselves. In doing this we risk losing whatever we refuse to share – because God's purpose is to bring light and life to this world, and whenever we prevent him from being what he has come to be, we fail to discover him as he really is. We are left with an empty shell of mere words and stories of past conquests.

A Festival of Rest and Worship
Our Western world has lost the ability to discern the things that are truly valuable. We pursue wealth, growth, material affluence and progress whilst trampling over the things that will make us truly happy and contented. And while this is happening, too much of the church is playing a Christianized version of the same game. I am convinced that nothing will change until Christians rediscover the meaning of God's command that we should rest and learn to enjoy all God has given.

The rest that God calls us to enjoy is based upon a renewed and refreshed relationship with him. It is about pausing and discovering that God is within us. It is an invitation to enjoy God and a chance to seek his blessing and his will. Without rest we are resisting God's will for our lives and are refusing to let him restore and remake us in his image. When we refuse to rest and enjoy God we are saying 'no' to his offer to show us how much he loves his children and are thus closing the door to the possibility of discovering the real meaning of 'special'. Like the brother of the Prodigal Son we are refusing to let God show us how to enjoy being redeemed people. As we rest we are also empowered and directed, because God is being given permission to re-order our priorities and help us see the world as it really is.

Rest was a part of the Sabbath day, the Sabbath year, Jubilee and all the annual festivals. Today we take our holidays, and perhaps our Sundays, off work; but we rarely *rest* in any true biblical sense. All too often our rest days are filled with more – admittedly different – activity. On Old Testament feast days, and on presenting the annual tithe the focus was never upon self-righteous giving, or on grudging obedience, but on joyful and generous partying. John Taylor comments that Deuteronomy 14 describes:

> a spending spree, whisky and all, to make our commercial Christmas look like a lenten fast! That was their way of saying thank you to God. Such spontaneous, lavish celebration is the absolute opposite of the greedy spirit of grasping, hoarding, exploiting and turning everything back into greater profits.[17]

To know God in our midst is to know life, and to know why to party. Harvest too was a similar type of celebration; a seven day holiday in which the people were instructed to come and enjoy God together and share their joy and their produce with each other.

How far we have fallen! How do our Harvest services with their displays of produce and well-worn harvest hymns and liturgies compare with this ideal? They do not. We must think again. If we are to succeed in breathing new life into the Harvest Festival we need to think radically and produce something very different – perhaps by turning it into either a weekend or even a week of celebrations? We may include Harvest Suppers – as some churches already do – but why stop there? Why not also plan home group celebrations or meals, put on Harvest suppers for the elderly, the children of the church, or a disadvantaged group in the community? And these Harvest Suppers would be a great deal more meaningful if the food to be eaten was donated by local farmers or grown in the allotments and gardens of church members. Or how about the church renting an allotment a year in advance and enabling its members to plant the food that was going to be needed for the supper. Why not consider throwing a party or some kind of dance – with the express purpose of thanking God for his goodness and for sins forgiven. And perhaps we might finance this kind of celebration by tithing church income or by encouraging individuals to do the same, bearing in mind Jesus' promise that whatever we give 'will be given to you. A good measure, pressed down, shaken together and running over will be poured into your lap.'[18] Who knows, this might even help us recover the practice of cheerful giving!

If harvest is to once again become a celebration of the goodness of creation it seems a commonsense suggestion that we should also consider making a greater effort to enjoy and experience the creation as we rest. Perhaps it seems a daft and unnecessary suggestion to many; but if we are to again become people who care for the creation in wise and just ways it is essential that we know how to enjoy and appreciate our beautiful world; and that we learn to appreciate its variety and inter-relatedness, and discover that it is there in all its glory whether we take the time to enjoy it or not. Time spent watching and studying the creation – whether on foot, in books or on television – restores a sense of awe to us that is so often lacking when we spend all our time in the artificial world we have created for ourselves. Time spent engaging with nature will also enable us to slow down to a more natural rhythm, and will help us attune our natural inner ear both to God and the world around us. It is far easier to offer meaningful worship to our creator when we have also taken the time to see and appreciate the beauty of all he has made.

All this is easy to suggest and read but will have little effect unless individuals take the initiative and do something. The best place to begin is with what already exists. Why not do some research amongst your congregation and discover which environmental projects or groups are already receiving their support? How about asking them to help produce a presentation or an information stand telling others about the work of the group they support? If there are several different nature interest or environmental campaigning groups represented there will be plenty of material for an evening gathering – perhaps including an opportunity for your activists to explain why they are involved as they are or a debate around a motion like 'This House believes that any action to improve our environment is simply delaying the return of Christ.' Such an event should have at least two benefits: it will help the environmentally concerned to affirm that their love for God's earth is not a 'secular' issue that has no place within a worshipping community; and it will challenge the rest of the congregation to tackle the issues of stewardship and also deepen their love for the God of creation. Such a presentation also makes an excellent evangelistic opportunity since, as Paul says in Romans 1: 'God's invisible qualities – his eternal power and divine nature – have been clearly seen, being understood from what has been made.' When he created the earth God was doing our pre-evangelism for us! Some years ago I was invited to help a group of Bible College students reflect on God's call to us to act as wise stewards alongside the fact that we are concerned about the state of our planet. Their aim was to build a presentation they could use on evangelistic missions run by the College.

If you can find no one who actively supports any group you will find a list of groups at the end of this chapter, together with contact addresses and websites in the Appendix. You will also find a list of possible sources of funding if you have a project of your own in mind. Or you could begin by discovering more about your immediate area. How about asking a church member to do some local research with the aim of discovering the variety of local parks, guided walks, nature trails, environmental projects etc. in your area? It is remarkable how many sites of great environmental interest we have all around us and how little we know about them. Many parks and projects also have staff who will conduct guided walks or produce information which will assist in enhancing your appreciation of each site. If you discover an environmental project in your area perhaps it would be possible to encourage a church group to give up some of their time and energy to help out in practical ways – assuming the work is not too specialized. Or maybe there are those in your congregation who are land users – farmers, smallholders, market gardeners etc. who have a land-management role of some kind. Might it be possible to enlist their help in planning an event, or even include a visit to their place of work in your harvest itinerary. Perhaps they could also help shape your Harvest worship service. If you live in a country area it may be possible to arrange a rogation-style walk around the boundaries of your parish – perhaps together with a group from the neighbouring parish. You could stop at various sites for prayer – thanking God for his goodness and asking him to bless all your eyes can see. It will probably be helpful to provide a few theological pointers to help those gathered to link the things they can see with God's requirements that we be wise stewards over creation.

When it comes to enjoying God at these festival times almost anything is possible. During the Feast of Tabernacles the Israelites built temporary booths to remind them of the time they spent in the wilderness. 'Tradition says they were to construct booths with enough spaces in the thatches so they could feel the wind blowing through and see the stars shining at night.'[19] They also waved branches to symbolize the fruits of harvest, and later at about the time of Jesus the Feast of Tabernacles would be marked by a trumpet blast at daybreak, a water pouring ceremony and a night-time torch dance in the

Court of Women. As I said, anything is possible! There has not been space here to include examples of any liturgical material. But since the most appropriate liturgical frameworks are often those that are designed locally this is probably not a bad thing. The Arthur Rank Centre have produced some helpful models for Plough Sunday, Rogation, Lammas and Harvest, all of which provide a good starting point, and the Report of the Conference on Environmental Issues in the Church of England (5 May 2000)[20] has some material used by the Bishop of Hereford. Much of the material from the Iona Community is also helpful if you come from a liturgical tradition. The Eco-Congregation project also has a module of worship ideas which include prayers, ideas for an All-Age service, drama material, reflections on bible stories and much more.

But amidst this festivity we must also create space – space for God to be himself and to meet with us. We have come to believe that with our agricultural and scientific expertise we can ensure plentiful harvests and can make everything we desire for ourselves. And we are right – in the material sense. But we are wrong if we assume we can be fulfilled without reference to God and his requirements and that the Old Testament festivals were just superstitious rituals to placate God and ensure good harvests. They were celebrations at which God's people declared their desire to walk with him and seek his blessing in all areas of their lives. It is this dimension we lack in our current age, and sadly the truth is that we have become used to spiritual poverty and now find it hard to imagine what life lived in the fulness of God's presence might be like. The truth is that all must be offered to God if we are to prosper in the things that matter and if God is going to be allowed to bless us. It would, perhaps, make sense to invigorate our traditional harvest displays with celebrations along the lines I have suggested, and then on the Sunday we could set time aside to seek God, to thank him in a more thoughtful way, to meditate on his promises and fix our eyes expectantly on what he wants to do with us in the future.

A Festival of Repentance

The bible is full of warnings against excess and constantly craving for more. In the Old Testament law we recall a command against covetousness,[21] whilst Jesus teaches that these desires for all kinds of excess come from within the heart of an unclean and empty person.[22] Paul tells God's people to put such cravings to death because they defile the very image of God Christ has come to renew.[23]

'The opposite of this lust for possession and domination is the readiness to fit one's own needs to the needs of others and to submit self-assertion to the claims of an equipoise society.'[24] The Greek word for moderation is *epieikes*, which Taylor shows has its roots in the word *ikon* and 'means a matching, a toning in with the whole, an awareness of how one's own small piece fits into the jigsaw picture.'[25] God's intention is to mould us into people who understand our place in the world so that we can appreciate the value of our surroundings and can begin to regain the kingdom of right relationships and a sense of accountability to God and to the whole of creation.

In Old Testament times it was the Festival of Trumpets that focused on repentance and the recognition of creation's goodness. Perhaps, in addition to renewing Harvest, we could also attempt a Christian recovery of New Year. Might it not be possible to spend the first Sunday of each New Year in celebration of God's goodness – not just for the things he has given us individually but also to recall the wonders of the world around us and remember our calling to be wise stewards. We should also recall our sin – both as individuals and as a society – and turn to God in repentance, resolving to do something to make a difference to our environment (either as a church or as families or individuals) during the coming year.

Harvest is rooted in the theology of 'enough' or of being satisfied with what we have, with its Old Testament roots in the lesson of the manna in Exodus 16. To reflect this, the congregation could spend time asking God to give them only what we need, and according to his wisdom.[26] The story speaks loudly to us when we read that each Israelite could gather all the food he needed, but when anyone gathered too much and tried hoarding it they discovered that by the morning it stank and was covered in maggots. Certainly this is the lesson that Paul teaches when he writes:

> Our desire is not that others might be relieved while you are hard pressed, but that there might be equality. At the present time your plenty will supply what they need so that in turn their plenty will supply what you need. Then there will be equality, as it is written: 'he that gathered much did not have too much, and he that gathered little did not have too little.'[27]

It is time we took this message to heart. I think we could make a start on this if at the beginning of each New Year we recalled the fact that everything we have comes from God and were determined to set our hearts only on those things which God wants to give us during the year ahead. These illustrations could be used as the basis for a New Year covenant in which we resolve to resist the pressure to buy more and more things we do not need. For some this will mean deliberately restricting our access to catalogues, magazines and brochures which so expertly aim to create a felt need to consume where there is actually no good reason for doing so. Contacting the Mailing Preference Service might be the first step to take in this.[28] Others will feel it necessary to put an end to the habit of comparing what they own with what others have, or reduce the number of trips into town to window-shop. The idea of a covenant is important since most of us find it easier to do what we know we should if we have planned our actions carefully and if we consider ourselves accountable in some way to do what we have planned. It may be a powerfully effective move to encourage members of existing Housegroups or Bible Study groups to help each other work out the personal details of this covenant before the service itself. This would also provide a ready-made support group for anyone who discovers they have become more dependent upon consumption than they had thought, and would enable the possibility of later review.

I should underline one potential danger at this point. It is important not to lose sight of the main objective by implying that it is consumption that is wrong and that we should be made to feel guilty for any pleasure we derive from enjoying the good things God has provided for us. The whole point of this exercise is to enable us to free ourselves from compulsive and unnecessary consumption so that we can then enjoy what we have more fully and devote more of our resources to worthier causes. A practical aid in this might be to make certain seldom-used items available to the rest of your Home Group, so every household doesn't need to own everything themselves. Alternatively a group could pool resources and buy items for common use.

Repentance involves the recognition of sin, confession and a determination to behave differently. Harvest was a popular and meaningful festival because it focused upon something nearly everyone did: farming the land and keeping animals. Despite the fact that most of us have little to do with our food production, most Harvest Festivals still concentrate on the harvest display in the laudable insistence that we should be as thankful for the food we buy from Sainsbury's as we would if we had grown it ourselves. But buying a few extra tins for a harvest display – and then creating the problem of what to do with all the food afterwards – is not the same as bringing first fruits at the beginning of Harvest and the best fruit at the end.

Our modern Harvest Festivals are token expressions of gratitude which actually do little to touch our lives.

But it seems important to me that harvest costs us something – not simply in symbolic terms but in a real, tangible way. Even giving a tenth of our income to God (if that is our practice) is not the same as giving first fruits to God. The Festival of Weeks came at the beginning of harvest, and a worshipper was not offering a proportion of his plenty, but the first part of a still awaited harvest. It was a gift in faith. It is all too easy for us to come to worship with the attitude that says 'how little can I get away with giving and still fulfil my requirements?' rather than 'what step of faith does God ask me to take?'[29] Perhaps a new kind of harvest could be an occasion when Christians dedicated their designated tithe to God. Or it could be a time for a special Gift Day – the proceeds of which could be given to those in real, absolute, need.

It might also be far more meaningful to organize a harvest display of talents, skills and professional services which members of both church and community could offer to give away to members of the community who cannot afford to pay for them. It would not be too difficult to liase with a range of local bodies who would be able to help with identifying the real needs of each community and could help put people in touch with each other. Surely an accountant offering an hour to help a disabled person work out her benefit entitlement is a legitimate modern equivalent of a worshipper bringing food to the Temple for the Levites to eat; and a housewife giving a few hours of her time to help clean for someone who cannot afford a home carer is today's equivalent of allowing a widow to glean the fields. This may take some time to put together, but would put the church in touch with the community, help meet real needs and, again, help eradicate that perceived divide between faith and practical action. If you discover that people are reticent to receive help without paying something for it, might it be possible to arrange an auction of volunteered services – with any money raised going to those in even greater need.

Another way we could use our talents to make a Harvest offering would be for a church to offer a small amount of money to anyone who will take it and is prepared to use it as capital to enable them to set up a money-making scheme. This capital would then be spent on buying raw materials to use in making something that could be sold at a profit so that this could then be re-invested and the process could begin again. At the end of the venture the capital sum could be returned and the profit donated to an environmental agency or a specific appeal, or the amount could be used as a hardship fund to benefit the needy – and would remain open for anyone to withdraw from to fund further schemes.

Another idea, which I have tried myself, is to promote a church-organized clean-up of a local beauty spot. This is an excellent way of giving expression to our theological convictions and bringing them to life. The great value of such initiatives is that they stick in the mind far longer than sermons and actually serve as permanent pegs to hang our theology on. However, I believe it is essential that a fellowship first begins with laying the theological foundations for such action, because without them it is hard to break down the barriers of reserve and laziness in a people who have grown too used to hearing God's word and doing little about it. Perhaps God's people have grown up believing that it is alright to preach about something and then do little in response because that is what our clergy-led and clergy-oriented ghettoes have modelled. If any of these pointers are going to work themselves out in practice in your locality it will be the church body that will supply the initiative and the drive – if they are allowed to do so. And this is the way it should be within the body of Christ. But church leaders must give a lead. Let me propose two ways in which we could do just that within our own fellowships: a local church ecological audit and a living churchyard project.

An Ecological Audit for the Local Church

This is an opportunity for those in charge of the church's facilities to submit themselves to an examination of the way things are done and to suggestions about how they might be done more efficiently in the future.

i. Is all church paperwork produced using recycled or reused paper?[30] Do you reuse envelopes or prefer to use manila envelopes which use less bleach?

ii. Is your church energy efficient?[31] Do you use low-energy light bulbs?

iii. Do you use glass and china rather than plastic or paper cups? Breaking the habits of a throwaway society has to begin somewhere and plastic is not easily bio-degradable.

iv. Do you use environment friendly cleaning products and recycled toilet paper?

v. Does your church recycle its waste paper, glass, aluminium and stamps, or could you do an important service to the community by operating your own recycling scheme or co-operating with an existing one?

vi. Do you encourage the sharing of cars where possible?

Decide on the measures you will take to improve your performance and make sure the decisions get communicated to those who are responsible.

The Living Churchyard Project

Just a few years ago the Arthur Rank Centre produced an excellent and very comprehensive resource entitled *The Living Churchyard*. It recognizes that in the many churchyards all around the country we have ideal opportunities to create areas of sanctuary for many endangered species.

What better place to demonstrate our care for creation and

understanding of this continuing stream of life? . . . In the way we care for churchyards we show our respect not only for the dead but for life and living things. Sadly many churchyards are managed in a way that is not hospitable to wildlife and offers no sanctuary. As Richard Mabey put it, 'At present churchyards are regarded principally as resting places for the dead, where a respectful sombre tidiness, clipped of the excesses of nature should prevail. That is an understandable feeling, but in the light of our growing sense of the interdependence of all life, a more hospitable reaction towards the rest of creation might be an apter Christian response.'[32]

The pack comes as part of a range of materials including a video, slide pack, and audio tape. Its six sections include extensive details of who is responsible for administering Church of England churchyards; information on different churchyard habitats; details of how to undertake a churchyard survey; management and planning techniques; information on books, organizations, resources, grants and insurance; and details on how to publicize your scheme and use it as an educational resource. For those churches (city or rural) with a churchyard to maintain this is an excellent place to begin.

A Festival of Justice
The Old Testament regulations on harvesting insist upon limited cropping to allow the poor a chance to glean from the corners of the fields and from the ears that were left behind after the first pass. They also allow the animals and land to rest on Sabbaths and during the prescribed fallow periods and state that there should be no planting between the lines (i.e. intensive farming). In addition, the Feast of Weeks and the tithe laws insisted that the first fruits were brought to God as an offering. All of these owe their existence to God's demand that humans should restrict their own freedom and act justly towards everyone and everything. So the law on limited

cropping was to ensure that the poor would be provided for, and was a restriction on greed. The command to rest and the prevention of dual cropping was to preserve the quality of the soil, and the bringing of the first fruits was a 'prohibition on snatching the chance of a high price because of the scarcity of the first fruits'.[33]

Our world has moved on a long way since those days. We are no longer an agriculturally based society, and the invention of the Welfare State in this country has meant that the problems these rules were given to solve may be met in other ways. We also need to recall that God gave these rules to a nation that professed to follow him. We cannot pretend that an unashamedly secular society such as our own enjoys the same covenant relationship with the creator of the universe. Since Christ established the New Covenant, the Church has become grafted into the people of God. It is therefore the Church that is expected to represent and respond to God.

But the demands of justice apply to all humanity. God's creation is under threat all over the world and there is still relative poverty in the West and absolute poverty in other countries. What is more, we are a notoriously greedy and self-satisfied country, and even if there were no social problems anywhere else in the world the Harvest restrictions would still go a long way towards saving us from ourselves if we took them seriously. Those of us who comprise the Church are called to live prophetically different lives so that we will be heard to call God's lost children to live according to the eternally wise principles of justice and righteousness. It is therefore important that our celebration of Harvest should include an element of prophetic initiative on behalf of the oppressed – either in our own land or elsewhere. Perhaps this is the hardest level at which to respond as individuals or churches. It is often assumed that such a call is more effective at a national or denominational level, but this need not be the case. Local initiatives – perhaps by groups of churches – are often more effective because more action is seen to be done. There are also things the individual can do – often locally – and since such action on behalf of others is in keeping with the spirit of Harvest, we can be assured that standing up for justice and alongside the oppressed will always have some significance even if little is achieved in terms of righting specific wrongs; because in doing so we are co-operating with the Spirit of God who is always at work in our world.

The 1992 Earth Summit in Rio de Janeiro led to an agreement by national governments to promote and support an initiative called Local Agenda 21. This recognizes that if we are to achieve sustainable development it is necessary to ensure that a strategy is developed. But it is of limited use to initiate a national strategy when the required action must involve partnerships between local government, businesses and voluntary groups at a local level. So Local Agenda 21 was a commitment by local authorities to undertake a consultative process and achieve a consensus on a 'local agenda 21' for their community by mid-1996. From that point all local authorities should have committed themselves to implementing specific programmes to improve the quality of the local environment, and be making arrangements to support local programmes that fit in with their declared strategy. This means that each of us has been presented with the opportunity (or responsibility) of approaching our local authority to find out the contents of its Local Agenda 21 and then asking how that strategy is being implemented and whether it presents us with any ideas as to how our churches can get involved. The great advantage of Local Agenda 21 is that since this is an already agreed strategy for improving the local environment, it may help us identify local needs we were previously unaware of and also carries the possibility of local authority funding.

Another issue which has become more prominent in recent

years is the drive to move towards the consumption of fairly traded goods. This initiative lends itself to church participation (and to the adoption of a church commitment to serve only fairly traded tea and coffee) and again provides a way of making more people aware of the injustices at the heart of the way we trade with developing nations. My own church has been holding Traidcraft fairs for many years (and even a clothes show) and these have become very popular in the community. Other churches take over empty shops in the pre-Christmas period and run short-term projects on the High Street. Contact Traidcraft or Tearcraft for more information about how you can help raise these issues and support their efforts to trade justly and speak on behalf of the world's poor.

Clearly there are numerous ways in which it is possible for us to expand our awareness of God's call upon us to live differently and care for all he has created. This is not a fringe issue, but goes to the heart of what is wrong with humanity. What is important now is that we allow God's calling to become so compelling that it provokes us to prayer, study and action. When it comes to taking action the most important thing is that we learn to commit ourselves to the things God is calling us to do and become the people he expecting us to be – in the recognition that justice is an incomplete concept unless it embraces a vision of complete shalom for the whole earth.

I have suggested that a natural way to return to a right appreciation of all God has given us is to renew the Harvest festival; and I have suggested a number of ways it could be made a more relevant and meaningful occasion. The suggestions I have made are only intended as seed thoughts. There must be many more possibilities. I have written all this in the conviction that we have been given the responsibility of caring for our world, and that we have moved too far from the cycle of festivals which underpinned Old and New Testament life. These two facts are not unconnected because, as I have shown, the festivals we have not replaced were the ones that had a distinctly stewardship-centred emphasis. So Harvest needs rescuing, and if this is going to happen it is essential that we give it back its theological base and make it more of a festival of Creation. It is also important that we find practical and relevant ways of presenting our tithes, first fruits and offerings to God. Theology that fills our heads and stays there is useless. It is only as we give practical expression to that theology that it will come alive and truly become part of us. As we act obediently we are also enabling this theology to take on an added depth and dimension. We must 'feel' our theology – both in rest and activity, and should be prepared to imaginatively examine every opportunity so that we can make Harvest a new festival for our modern age.

Finally, I want to introduce you to a number of groups[34] which may offer you further opportunities or ideas as you seek to make your commitment to stewardship practical:

A Rocha

The A Rocha Trust was founded in 1983 and is committed to mission through Christian witness on environmental matters. A Rocha describes itself under the following headings:

- Christian: we are motivated by our biblical faith, particularly in God the Creator
- Conservation: we focus on scientific studies of important habitats and species
- Community: we bring people together for environmental education and action, with special emphasis on students and school children
- Cross-cultural: we involve staff and volunteers inter-nationally and give priority to parts of the world where resources for conservation and Christian witness are limited
- Campaigning: we work with local and international agencies for the protection of key areas and environments

208

A Rocha seeks to achieve its objectives by:

- Educating young people. This is because they are key to changing attitudes – which is a priority for A Rocha. They train volunteers in order to spread good conservation practices, especially in parts of the world where conservation principles are not well understood or practiced.
- A Rocha seeks to prioritize high-quality scientific research, so its conservation recommendations to governments and local authorities are well informed and accurate.
- Strategy Priority is given to places where interest and resources about conservation are limited. A Rocha demonstrates practical results through field centres that are located in threatened habitats.
- A Rocha aims to work with local and international agencies in order to achieve maximum effectiveness in the protection of key habitats

The Trust began in 1983 by establishing a field centre and bird observatory in South West Portugal. This has now been visited by thousands of people from around the world and has helped train over 500 volunteers, many of whom are still active in conservation work. They now have a database which holds records of over 58,000 birds ringed, whilst extensive studies of plants and fungi, moths and butterflies have given a firm basis for influential reports and articles on the Algarve environment. Proposals for increased legal protection for the Alvor estuary stem directly from A Rocha's studies.

This was followed by a project in the Bekaa valley in 1997, which aims to protect the last significant wetland in Lebanon. This important site is under threat from drainage and conversion into agricultural land, and has been damaged by fires, overgrazing, pollution and general disturbance. As a result of the A Rocha initiative, the landowners have agreed to the creation of a nature reserve and have given space in a nearby stable that has become an education and interpretation centre. A programme of visits by schools and university groups has also been established.

A Rocha are currently working with French conservationists and church leaders towards identifying a suitable site for a project in that country, and have also recently launched Living Waterways – A Rocha's first UK project, and the first project in an urban setting, working with the religiously and culturally diverse populations of Southall and Hayes in West London. The long-term aim is to set up a nature reserve and linked environmental education centre on derelict, partly-contaminated land between the Grand Union Canal and the Yeading Brook. In the medium term they are working with schools and community groups in curriculum-based activities, after-school clubs, and playschemes to raise environmental awareness and concern, and plan to have a floating classroom in a narrowboat on the canal! A national association has also been established in Kenya, and plans for a centre are well advanced. In Canada the national association has begun a series of activities and there is active interest in similar initiatives in the Czech Republic, Brazil, and more recently Ghana and India.

A Rocha produces an annual pack of materials for worship, bible study and practical action. It is produced in time for Conservation Sunday – the first Sunday in June each year, to coincide with the Wildlife Trusts' 'Wildlife Week', but it is designed to be flexible and can be used at any time.

A membership scheme was started in the UK in 1996 and has already grown to over 1000 members. The main objective of the scheme is to spread the vision of A Rocha. National membership schemes are planned in a number of other countries.

The Arthur Rank Centre

The Arthur Rank Centre is an independent institution working on a number of initiatives relating to rural affairs, and houses the Rural Affairs Officer for the Church of England.

The Church and Conservation Project started the Living Churchyard project which now has some 6000 burial grounds in approved environmental management. Information is available on various technical aspects such as Birds in Churchyards, Dry Stone Walls, Geology, Trees and Hedges, Butterflies and Lichens. More recently an award winning pack for schools (Keystage 2) called Hunt the Daisy has been published.

The Arthur Rank Centre seeks to encourage the thousands of farmers who already participate in Farming and Wildlife Advisory Group (FWAG) projects or on Linking Environment And Farming (LEAF) farms, and helps those involved in the countryside to consider the ethical issues over issues such as GM crops. They are also seeking to publicize the new Local Heritage Initiative in rural churches, since it offers the chance to show how local churches care for the environment.

The Centre believes the best way to preserve our old churches is to use them more. Thus it supports the objectives of the Open Churches Trust, the Council for the Care of Churches and others for greater access, better presentation of the buildings and more partnership in the business of ministering to visitors. The Rural Churches in Community Service is currently allocating a grant of £2.5m from the Millennium Commission to 100 churches to help them adapt the premises to meet the needs of the contemporary community. Care for the environment often goes hand in glove with care for the most needy in society.

Christian Ecology Link

Christian Ecology Link is an ecumenical organization committed to taking care of God's creation. Formed in 1981, its primary aim is to encourage Christians to integrate awareness of their impact on the environment into their faith and lifestyles.

CEL has produced a wide range of leaflets and other resources and publishes its *Green Christians* magazine and a news sheet for display in churches (ChurchLink). They also maintain a web site which has over 100 pages and is updated each week.

CEL has links with the major churches through denominational teams, and are represented on the Environmental Issues Network and are also active in the European Christian Environmental Network. Periodically CEL issues statements on key environmental issues, attracting publicity in national newspapers and the church press.

In recent years CEL has increasingly sought to provide support and resources to individuals seeking to influence others within their church. They provide resources to help churches undertake environmental audits and Harvest worship services, alongside suggested Christian responses on a variety of topics and information about planting trees to commemorate special events. More recently CEL has presented Millennium Certificates to churches that select and undertake ten activities to reduce their environmental impact. This approach has proved very successful, as it is not prescriptive and can therefore be adapted to individual churches' capabilities and needs.

CEL convenes events at both a national and a local level. There is an annual meeting for members and local groups in some areas.

Eco-Congregation

Eco-Congregation developed from a partnership between the environmental awareness charity 'Going for Green' and the Environmental Issues Network of what is now Churches Together in Britain and Ireland. Their Project Officer's main

task is to develop and manage an Eco-Congregation programme which was launched in September 2000.
Eco-Congregation aims:

- To encourage, enable and excite local congregations to rejoice in God's gift of creation through worship, and to care for this gift in every aspect of their life.
- To encourage congregations to become beacons of environmental excellence and social care, both in their local community and for their local community.
- To encourage and enable the church at regional, national and international levels to make positive responses to environmental issues.

An initial Pilot Study was launched to discover what form of resources would be most helpful for churches and what they could achieve which would aid the development of an Award to recognize achievement. It also sought to test how it could promote Eco-Congregation and support churches in their endeavours

The Pilot Study involved 22 churches, representing 8 denominations, from across England, Wales, Scotland and Northern Ireland. Churches varied in size from 10 to around 1,000 members and were drawn from urban, suburban and rural areas with a variety of cultural contexts. In less than six months, participating churches had managed to undertake a wide and inspiring range of practical and spiritual activities, including:

- Conducting an environmental audit;
- Conducting a 'creation-centred' worship service;
- Recycling a range of materials;
- 'Freighting and crating' old tools to Africa;
- Practical conservation work;
- Working with a basket weaver to teach children the story of Moses in the rushes;

- Establishing a policy to promote the use of eco-friendly cleaning materials.

Churches also reported that in addition to the range of positive achievements, tackling environmental issues had been both stimulating and fun and had a number of other positive spin-offs. It gave a focus to church life, improved fellowship and led to new links with community groups and local authorities.

A set of eco-congregation study modules has been created and are available free of charge. They cover the following areas:

- Churches Check-up: an environmental audit, helping to assess a church's current environmental practice and identify priorities for action
- Celebrating Creation: Resources and ideas for Worship
- Creation and Christianity: Theological reflections
- Acorns to Oaks: Ideas and activities for Children's work
- Tread Gently: Ideas and activities for Youth Work
- Exploring God's green world: Bible Studies for House Groups
- Greening the Cornerstone: Management of church buildings
- Greening the purse-strings: Management of financial, purchasing and catering matters
- Planting and conserving Eden: Ideas for church land and gardens
- Green Choices: Personal lifestyle issues
- Community Matters: Ideas to help churches work with, through and for their local community
- Global Neighbours: Sources and resources to help churches think globally and act locally.

Eco-Congregation is promoted nationally, regionally and locally. The Project Officer is developing and managing Eco-Congregation by focusing his work upon encouraging 'Green Intermediaries' working in regions or local authority areas.

The Green Intermediaries will encourage churches in their area to get involved in environmental issues and enable them to respond in both practical and spiritual ways.

The Green Apostles are appointed by their own church to co-ordinate and oversee their green activities. Green Apostles are encouraged to form a 'green team' to support their church's work

An Eco-Congregation Award Scheme is being developed to act as a target for churches; recognize and affirm positive achievements; witness that the church is taking environmental issues seriously; and provide a feedback and evaluation mechanism. The Eco-Congregation Award will recognize both the way that a church approaches environmental issues and the creditable achievements that it makes. The Award will be assessed independently, with a minimum of two judges drawn from church, local authority and environmental networks and winners will be given a banner in recognition of their achievements.

Environmental Issues Network

The Environmental Issues Network was established in 1990. It aims to draw representatives from the churches in membership of Churches Together in Britain and Ireland and other Christian organizations, in order to consider environmental and ecological issues. It meets three times a year.

EIN acts to exchange news and information, to promote co-operation and avoid wasteful duplication of effort. Its members reflect and comment on specific environmental issues.

The John Ray Initiative

The John Ray Initiative was begun by a group of leading Christian scientists in 1997 in order to bring together scientific and Christian understandings of the environment in a way that can be widely communicated and lead to effective action. It aims to promote a deeper understanding of the environment and show how observation and study can produce an ethical approach to decision making and stewardship.

Drawing inspiration from John Ray, the seventeenth century Christian who saw scientific enquiry as a form of worship, the JRI seeks to:

- Demonstrate and teach the wonder of nature, including its diversity and complexity.
- Increase awareness of environmental harm resulting from human failure to be good stewards.
- Encourage responsible stewardship and stimulate the development of Christian understanding of the environment and the way in which human society interacts with it.
- Demonstrate and teach how the natural and social sciences and technology can be harnessed to protect the environment and ameliorate environmental damage.
- Stimulate local, national and international action in pursuit of environmental protection and sustainable development.
- Encourage and co-operate with Christian environmental initiatives.
- Demonstrate good environmental stewardship in the way they work.

JRI seeks to discover and communicate an authentically Christian understanding of the environment through Theological Consultations with other organizations, speaking at conferences and churches, writing briefs and papers, and via its website, where information, briefing papers and educational resources can also be found. It is also building a team of Accredited Associates who will represent JRI at regional events and by providing resource materials.

Notes

1. Numbers 9:7.
2. 2 Kings 22-23; Nehemiah 8-10; Isaiah 1:13-20; Nahum 1:15.
3. Acts 20:16.
4. I acknowledge the help of The Arthur Rank Centre for providing me with much of the background material for these pen sketches. Their booklet *Church Services for the Farming Year for Town and Country* provides much helpful liturgical material.
5. William Dumbrell. *Covenant and Creation. An Old Testament Covenantal Theology* (Paternoster. Exeter. 1984) p 116.
6. Leviticus 25:23.
7. Deuteronomy 26:11.
8. Numbers 13:27.
9. Dumbrell. op. cit. (1984) p 120.
10. Ibid. p 121-122.
11. Ibid. p 122.
12. Ibid.
13. Judges 21:25.
14. Genesis 12:1-3.
15. John 1:29.
16. John 3:16.
17. John Taylor – *Enough is Enough.* (SCM Press. London. 1975) p 61.
18. Luke 6:38.
19. Barry Leisch – *People in the Presence of God: Models and Directions for Worship.* (Highland. Crowborough. 1990) p 227.
20. Environmental Issues in the Church of England. Report of the Conference on May 25th 2000. C of E Board of Social Responsibility.
21. Exodus 20:17.
22. Mark 7:21.
23. Colossians 3:5.
24. Taylor. op. cit. (1975) p 45.
25. Ibid. p 45-6.
26. James 4:3.
27. 2 Corinthians 8:13-15.
28. The Mailing Preference Service, Freepost 22, London W1E 7EZ will request their members to remove your name from junk mail lists.
29. In the spirit of Hebrews 11:6
30. A list of suppliers of recycled paper can be found by contacting The Association of Recycled Paper Suppliers, Bow Triangle Business Centre, Unit 2, Eleanor Street, London. E3 4NP.
31. The Church of Scotland have produced two reports on energy saving measures for churches: *Make the Most of it* and *Make Even More of it.* They are available from Church of Scotland SRT Project, 121 George Street, Edinburgh.

217

32. From the Introduction to *The Living Churchyard.*
33. Taylor. op. cit. (1975) p 54.
34. Much of the information on the various groups is taken from the 'Environmental Resources' section of the *Environmental Issues in the Church of England* booklet.

Appendix

Useful Addresses

A Rocha

International office:
A Rocha International Administrator
Connansknowe
Kirkton, Dumfries DG1 1SX
a_rocha@compuserve.com

A Rocha UK
13 Avenue Road
Southall, Middlesex UB1 3BL
David.bookless@care4free.net

Arthur Rank Centre

Revd Jeremy Martineau
The National Agricultural Centre
Stoneleigh Park
Warwickshire CV8 2LZ
j.martineau@ruralnet.org.uk

Association of
Recycled Paper
Suppliers

Bow Triangle Business Centre
Unit 2, Eleanor Street
London E3 4NP

Christian Ecology Link

George Dent
CEL Information Officer
20 Carlton Road, Harrogate
North Yorkshire HG2 8DD
info@christian-ecology.org.uk
www.christian-ecology.org.uk

Conservation
Foundation

1 Kensington Gore
London SW7 2AR
conservef@gn.apc.org
www.conservationfoundation.co.uk

Eco-Congregation

David Pickering
Going for Green
Elizabeth House
The Pier, Wigan WN3 4EX
david@tidybritain.org.uk

Environmental
Investigation Agency

208/9 Upper Street
London, N1 1RL

Environmental Issues
Network

Quarfseter,
4 Sackville Close
Sevenoaks, Kent
TN13 3QD

Friends of the Earth

26-28 Underwood Street
London N1 7JQ

Greenpeace

Canonbury Villas
London N1 2PN

John Ray Initiative

Room TC 103
Francis Close Hall
Cheltenham & Gloucester
College of FE
Swindon Road
Cheltenham GL50 4AZ
jri@chelt.ac.uk
www.jri.org.uk

Local Agenda 21   Local Government
                   Management Board
                   Arndale House
                   The Arndale Centre
                   Luton
                   Bedfordshire LU1 2TS

Mailing Preference   Freepost 22
Service   London W1E 7EZ

SRT Project   Society, Religion and
               Technology Project
               Church of Scotland
               John Knox House
               45 High Street, Edinburgh EH1 1SR
               srtp@srtp.org.uk
               www.srtp.org

Information on Fair Traded Goods
Traidcraft   Kingsway, Gateshead
              Tyne and Wear NE11 0NE

Oxfam Trading   Murdoch Road, Bicester
                 Oxon OX6 6RF

Christian Aid   PO Box 100
                 London SE1 7RT

The Fairtrade   7th Floor, Regent House
Foundation   89 Kingsway, London WC2B 6RH

Sources of Project Funding

There are many possible sources of advice and funding for local projects. It would make sense to make contact with the person responsible for Social Issues within your denomination (if applicable) and local businesses which may set aside grants for local charitable projects.

The Heritage Lottery Fund is the main contributor to environmental projects amongst the Lottery distribution bodies, but many churches have good reasons for refusing to apply for this money.

National Lotteries Charities Board
16 Suffolk Street
London SW1Y 4NL
www.nlcb.org.uk

The Landfill Tax Credit Scheme is an arrangement whereby waste disposal companies pay up to 20 per cent of the tax charged by the Inland Revenue into funding for environmental activities. Grants are administered either by the landfill operator or associated charitable bodies set up for this task. More information is available from:

ENTRUST,
154 Buckingham Palace Road
London SW1 9TR

If you live in a rural area, Rural Action will help with grants of up to half the cost of your project and will offer specialist advice, technical services and training.

Rural Action National Team
ACRE, Somerford Court
Somerford Road
Cirencester
Gloucestershire GL7 1TW

English Nature is committed to helping you to get enjoyment from nurturing local wildlife by creating or maintaining local wild places in urban areas.

Grants Officer
English Nature
Northminster House
Peterborough
Northamptonshire PE1 1UA

The Shell Better Britain Campaign provides a free Campaign guide full of advice and information to help you with planning a project and details of grant givers.

Arts & Environmental Sponsorship
Shell-Mex House
Strand
London WC2R 0DX

The Environmental Funding Guide (Susan Forrester and Dave Casson. Directory of Social Change. 1998. ISBN 1 900360 21 7) gives more details of the above, and comprehensive details of numerous different sources of further funding. It also contains advice about the kinds of projects preferred by each body and trusts with particular geographical areas of interest.

Bibliography

Books

Richard Bauckham	*Moltmann. Messianic Theology in the Making.*	Marshall Pickering. Basingstoke. 1987.
Sam Berry	*Ecology and Ethics.*	IVP. Leicester. 1989.
Charles Birch et. al.	*Liberating Life.*	Orbis. Maryknoll, New York. 1990.
Steve Bishop and Christopher Droop	*The Earth is the Lord's.*	Regius. Bristol. 1990.
Henri Blocher	*In the Beginning.*	IVP. Leicester. 1984.
George Caird	*Principalities and Powers: A Study in Pauline Theology.*	Clarendon Press. Oxford. 1954.
Tim Cooper	*Green Christianity.*	Hodder & Stoughton. London. 1990.
Stephen Davis (ed.)	*Encountering Evil: Live options in Theodicy.*	T & T Clark. Edinburgh. 1981.
Calvin DeWitt (ed.)	*The Environment and the Christian. What Does the New Testament say about the Environment?*	Baker Book House. Grand Rapids, Michigan. 1991.
W. Dumbrell	*Covenant and Creation. An Old Testament Covenantal Theology.*	Paternoster. Exeter. 1984.
Edward Echlin	*The Green Christian Heritage.*	Grove. Nottingham. 1989.
Ron Elsdon	*Bent World. Science, the Bible and the Environment.*	IVP. Leicester. 1981.
Ron Elsdon	*Greenhouse Theology. Biblical Perspectives on Caring for Creation.*	Monarch. Speldhurst, Kent. 1992.
David Gosling	*A New Earth – Covenanting for Justice, Peace and the Integrity of Creation.*	CCBI. London. 1992.

Wesley Granberg Michaelson (ed.)	*Tending the Garden.*	Eerdmans. Grand Rapids, Michigan. 1987.
Mary Grey	*The Wisdom of Fools? Seeking Revelation for Today.*	SPCK. London. 1993.
Catherina Halkes	*New Creation. Christian Feminism and the Renewal of the Earth.*	SPCK. London. 1991.
Douglas John Hall	*Imaging God. Dominion as Stewardship.*	Friendship Press. New York. 1986.
Douglas John Hall	*The Steward. A Biblical Symbol Come of Age.*	Eerdmans. Grand Rapids, Michigan. 1990.
George Hendry	*Theology of Nature.*	Westminster Press. Philadelphia. 1980.
Dieter Hessel (ed.)	*After Nature's Revolt. Eco-Justice and Theology.*	Fortress Press. Minneapolis, Minnesota. 1992.
James Houston	*I Believe in the Creator.*	Eerdmans. Grand Rapids, Michigan. 1980.
Keith Innes	*Caring for the Earth – The Environment, Christians and the Church.*	Grove. Nottingham. 1987.
Barry Leisch	*People in the Presence of God: Models and Directions for Worship.*	Highland. Crowborough E. Sussex. 1990.
Andrew Linzey and Tom Regan	*Animals and Christianity.*	SPCK. London. 1988.
David Livingstone	*Darwin's Forgotten Defenders: The Encounter between Evangelical Theology and Evolutionary Thought.*	Eerdmans. Grand Rapids, Michigan. 1987.
Sean McDonagh	*The Greening of the Church.*	Chapman. London. 1986.
Paulos Mar Gregorios	*The Human Presence. An Orthodox view of Nature.*	WCC. Geneva. 1978.
Timothy Marks	*His Light in Our Darkness.*	Kingsway. Eastbourne. 1988.

E.L. Mascall	*Christian Theology and Natural Science.*	Longmans. London. 1956.
Jürgen Moltmann	*God in Creation.*	SCM. London. 1985.
Jürgen Moltmann	*Theology of Hope.*	SCM. London. 1967.
Jürgen Moltmann	*The Crucified God. The Cross as the Foundation and Criticism of Christian Theology.*	SCM. London. 1974.
Hugh Montefiore (ed.)	*Man and Nature.*	Collins. London. 1975.
James Moore	*The Post-Darwinian Controversies: A study of the Protestant struggle to come to terms with Darwin in Great Britain and America 1870-1900.*	Cambridge University Press. Cambridge. 1979.
Rowland Moss	*The Earth in Our Hands.*	IVP. Leicester. 1982.
Lawrence Osborn	*Meeting God in Creation.*	Grove. Nottingham. 1990.
Chris Park	*Caring for Creation.*	Marshalls. London. 1992.
John Passmore	*Man's responsibility for Nature – Ecological problems and Western Traditions.*	Scribner. New York. 1974.
John Piper	*Future Grace.*	IVP. Leicester. 1995.
John Polkinghorne	*Science and Christian Belief. Theological Reflections of a bottom-up thinker.*	SPCK. London. 1994.
Colin A. Russell	*Crosscurrents: Interactions Between Science and Faith.*	IVP. Leicester. 1985.
H. Paul Santmire	*The Travail of Nature.*	Fortress Press. Minneapolis, Minnesota. 1985.
Francis Schaeffer	*Pollution and the Death of Man – The Christian view of Ecology.*	Tyndale. Wheaton, Illinois. 1970.
Francis Schaeffer	*Genesis in Space and Time.*	IVP. Downers Grove. Illinois. 1972.
Philip Sherrard	*The Rape of Man and Nature.*	Golgonooza Press. 1987.

Bibliography

Kathryn Tanner	*God and Creation in Christian Theology.*	Blackwell. Oxford. 1988.
John Taylor	*Enough is Enough.*	SCM. London. 1975.
A.N. Triton	*Whose World?*	IVP. Leicester. 1970.
Leonard Verduin	*Somewhat less than God: The Biblical view of Man.*	Eerdmans. Grand Rapids, Michigan. 1970.
Alec Vidler	*The Church in an Age of Revolution. 1789 to the present day.*	Penguin. London. 1971.
Andrew Walker	*Different Gospels. Christian Orthodoxy and Modern Theologies. (Revised Edition)*	SPCK. London. 1993.
Walsh and Middleton	*The Transforming Vision.*	IVP. Leicester. 1984.
Claus Westermann	*Creation.*	SPCK. London. 1974
Robert Whelan	*Mounting Greenery.*	IEA. London. 1989.
Loren Wilkinson	*Earthkeeping in the Nineties.*	Eerdmans. Grand Rapids, Michigan. 1992.
Albert Wolters	*Creation Regained.*	Eerdmans. Grand Rapids, Michigan. 1985.
Christopher Wright	*Living as the People of God. The Relevance of Old Testament Ethics.*	IVP. Leicester. 1983.

Commentaries

David Atkinson	*The Message of Genesis.*	IVP. Leicester. 1990.
C.E.B. Cranfield	*Romans. A Shorter Commentary.*	Eerdmans. Grand Rapids, Michigan. 1985.
Derek Kidner	*Genesis.*	IVP. Leicester. 1967.
Gerhard von Rad	*Genesis.*	SCM. London. 1972.
Claus Westermann	*Genesis 1-11.*	SPCK. London. 1984.
John Ziesler	*Paul's letter to the Romans.*	SCM. London. 1989.

Articles

Günter Altner	The Community of Creation as a Community in Law. The New Contract between the Generations.	*Concilium.* 1991/4. SCM Press. ed. Johann Baptist Metz & Edward Schillebeeckx.
A. Hilary Armstrong	The World in God.	*M C* Vol xxxiv No 1. Manchester. 1992.
James Barr	Man and Nature – The Ecological Controversy and the Old Testament.	*Bulletin of the John Rylands Library of Manchester.* Vol 55. Autumn 1972. No 1.
Sam Berry	Christianity and the Environment. Escapist Mysticism or Responsible Stewardship.	*Science and Christian Belief.* 1991. 3, 3-18.
Sam Berry	Environmental knowledge, attitudes and action. A code of practice.	*Scientific Public Affairs.* 5(2). 13-23. 1990.
John Biggs	Order and Chaos.	*Theology Themes.* Northern Baptist College. Manchester. Spring 1992.
Stephen Bishop	Towards a Biblical View of Environmental Care.	*Evangel.* Summer 1989.
Stephen Bishop	Green Theology and Deep Ecology. New Age or New Creation?	*Themelios.* April/May 1991 Vol. 16. No. 3.
Ian Bradley	A Glimpse of God's Mystery.	The *Guardian.* Oct 9 1991.
Susan Bratton	Christian Ecotheology and the Old Testament.	*Environmental Ethics.* Fall 1984. Vol 6. No 3.
Susan Bratton	Loving Nature. Eros or Agape?	*Environmental Ethics.* Spring 1992. Vol. 14. No 1.
Susan Bratton	The Original Desert Solitaire. Early Christian Monasticism and Wilderness.	*Environmental Ethics.* Spring 1988. Vol 10. No 1.

Bibliography

Mark Brett	Motives and Intentions in Genesis 1.	*Journal of Theological Studies.* NS. Vol 42. Pt 1. April 1991. OUP.
Roger Burggraeve	Responsibility for a 'New Heaven and a New Earth'	*Concilium* 1991/4. SCM Press. ed. Johann Baptist Metz & Edward Schillebeeckx
Denis Carroll	A Green Theology? Theology and Ecology.	*The Way.* Vol 31. Oct 1991. No 4.
James Crampsey	Look at the birds of the air . . . Oct 1991. No 4.	*The Way.* Vol 31.
André Dumas	The Ecological Crisis and the Doctrine of Creation.	*The Ecumenical Review.* Vol XXVII, No 1. Jan 1975. WCC.
Alexandre Ganoczy	Ecological Perspectives in the Christian Doctrine of Creation.	*Concilium.* 1991/4. SCM Press. ed. Johann Baptist Metz & Edward Schillebeeckx
Susan Gillingham	Who makes the morning darkness? – God and Creation in the Book of Amos.	*Scottish Journal of Theology.* Vol 45. No 2. T&T Clark. Edinburgh. 1992.
David Gosling	Towards a Credible Ecumenical of Nature.	*The Ecumenical Review.* Vol 38. No 3. July 1986.
Walter Gulick	The Bible and Ecological Spirituality.	*Theology Today.* July 1991.
Will Hoyt	Finding God in the Death of Nature.	*New Oxford Review.* July/August 1991.
Fisher Humphreys	All Creatures of our God and King.	*Beeson College.* Birmingham, Alabama. 1990.
Daphne Hampson	The Theological Implications of a Feminist Ethic.	*M C* xxxi. No 1. Manchester. 1989.

J. Hurst	Towards a Theology of Conservation.	*Theology.* Vol LXXV. April 1972. No 622.
Jeanne Kay	Concepts of Nature in the Hebrew Bible.	*Environmental Ethics.* Winter 1988. Vol 10. No 4.
Werner Kroh	Foundations and Perspectives for an Ecological Ethics. The Problem of Responsibility for the Future as a Challenge to Theology.	*Concilium.* 1991/4. SCM Press. ed. Johann Baptist Metz & Edward Schillebeeckx.
Tim Marks	Wholeness.	*Evangel.* Summer 1989.
Richard Means	Why Worry about Nature?	Reproduced in *Pollution and the Death of Man.*
John Milbank	Out of the Greenhouse	New Blackfriars. Oxford. January 1993.
Rowland Moss	The Ethical Underpinnings of Man's Management of Nature.	*Faith and Thought.* Vol. iii No 1. 1985.
Ghillean and Anne Prance	The Environmental Crisis. A challenge to the Judeo-Christian Faith.	Details unavailable.
Ghillean Prance	Giver of Life – Sustain your Creation.	*International Review of Mission.*
Anne Primavesi	Attending and Tending.	*The Way.* Vol 31. Oct 1991. No 4.
Anne Primavesi	The Part for the Whole? An Ecofeminist Enquiry.	*Theology.* Vol XCIII. No 755. SPCK. Sept 1990.
Tim O'Riordan	Environmentalism.	*Environmental Cognition.*
Richard Russell	The Ecological Orientation of the Christian Faith.	*Biblical Creation.* 5.15 & 5.16.
H. Paul Santmire	Reflections on the Alleged Theological Bankruptcy of Western Theology.	*Anglican Theological Review.* Vol 57. No. 2 April 1975.
Bron Taylor	The Religion and Politics of Earth First!	*The Ecologist.* Vol 21 No 6. Nov/Dec 1991.

Bibliography

F. Wellbourn	Man's Dominion.	*Theology.* Vol LXXVIII. Nov. 1975. No 665. SPCK.
Lynn White Jr.	The Historical Roots of our Ecologic Crisis.	*Science.* 10 March 1967. Vol 155. No 3767.
Lynn White Jr.	The Future of Compassion.	*The Ecumenical Review.* Vol. 30. No 2. April 1978.